FAITH IN HERITAGE

Displacement, Development, and Religious Tourism in Contemporary China

Robert J. Shepherd

Routledge
Taylor & Francis Group
LONDON AND NEW YORK

First published 2013 by Left Coast Press, Inc.

Published 2016 by Routledge
2 Park Square, Milton Park, Abingdon, Oxon OX14 4RN
711 Third Avenue, New York, NY 10017, USA

Routledge is an imprint of the Taylor & Francis Group, an informa business

Library of Congress Cataloging-in-Publication Data:

Shepherd, Robert J., 1958-
Faith in heritage : displacement, development, and religious tourism in contemporary China/Robert J. Shepherd.
p. cm. — (Heritage, tourism, and community; vol. 6.)
Includes bibliographical references and index.
ISBN 978-1-61132-073-2 (hardback : alk. paper) — ISBN 978-1-61132-074-9 (pbk. : alk. paper) — ISBN 978-1-61132-075-6 (institutional eBook) — ISBN 978-1-61132-655-0 (consumer eBook)
1. Tourism—Religious aspects—China—Wutai Mountains. 2. Tourism—Religious aspects—Buddhism. 3. Buddhist pilgrims and pilgrimages—China—Wutai Mountains. 4. Heritage tourism—China—Wutai Mountains. 5. World heritage areas—China—Wutai Mountains. 6. Wutai Mountains (China)—Religious life and customs. 7. Wutai Mountains (China)—Social life and customs. I. Title.
G155.C55S574 2012
915.1′ 17—dc23
2012023806

ISBN 978-1-61132-073-2 hardback
ISBN 978-1-61132-074-9 paperback

Contents

Icon (above): Signboard at the Mount Wutai National Park Visitor Center construction site, 2012. It promotes Mount Wutai as an international destination famed for its material culture, natural scenery, and leisure activities. Yet the area's real fame is as a Buddhist pilgrimage site.

This book is dedicated to my parents, John and Corrine Shepherd.
They raised eight children with a lot of hard work and smiles and
always have encouraged us to be the best we can, whatever our choices.
The way they have lived has shown us how to be better people.
Thank you.

And in loving memory of Elli Dumont, I raise my glass.

Illustrations

Figures

Tables

Preface

Like most field work practitioners, I have struggled with the twin peaks of life as an academic—family and work obligations. Once gainfully employed, a settled life leads to family ties and work responsibilities, making it difficult for an anthropologist to spend a year in the field. I have been very fortunate in both regards. First, my partner, Fithri Diah Ekawati, has never begrudged my occasional absences. And second, the good people at George Washington University's Sigur Center for Asian Studies provided summer funding for my field research at Wutai Shan for four years, from 2008 until 2011. While certainly not the same experience as one gains through a long-term continuous presence at a site, this method of repeated visits necessitated by my life as a full-time teacher has given me insight into the ongoing transformation of Wutai Shan and hopefully something to say about this process in this book.

My debts and obligations run deep. I am grateful to Helaine Silverman of the University of Illinois for her advice, suggestions, and willingness to include this book in the series she edits on heritage for Left Coast Press. My colleagues Eyal Aviv, Kang Xiaofei, Shawn McHale, Ed McCord, and Deepa Ollapally served as listening boards for my ideas and sagely voices of productive questioning and insight. My field collaborators Gu Huimin and Larry Yu made my analysis of visitor motivations possible. Li Zheng, Zhang Yueyang, and Peter Chiang provided translation help, while Chris Wong, Winnie Nham, Josie Keller, Kyle Churchman, and Matt Grieger have been amiable office mates.

Sections of Chapter II appeared in *Heritage and Society* 2:1 (2009), 55–79, while parts of Chapter V were published in *Tourism Management* 32:1 (2011), 187–190. A substantially different version of Chapter IV appeared in the *Journal of Heritage Tourism* 7:2 (2012), 145–161.

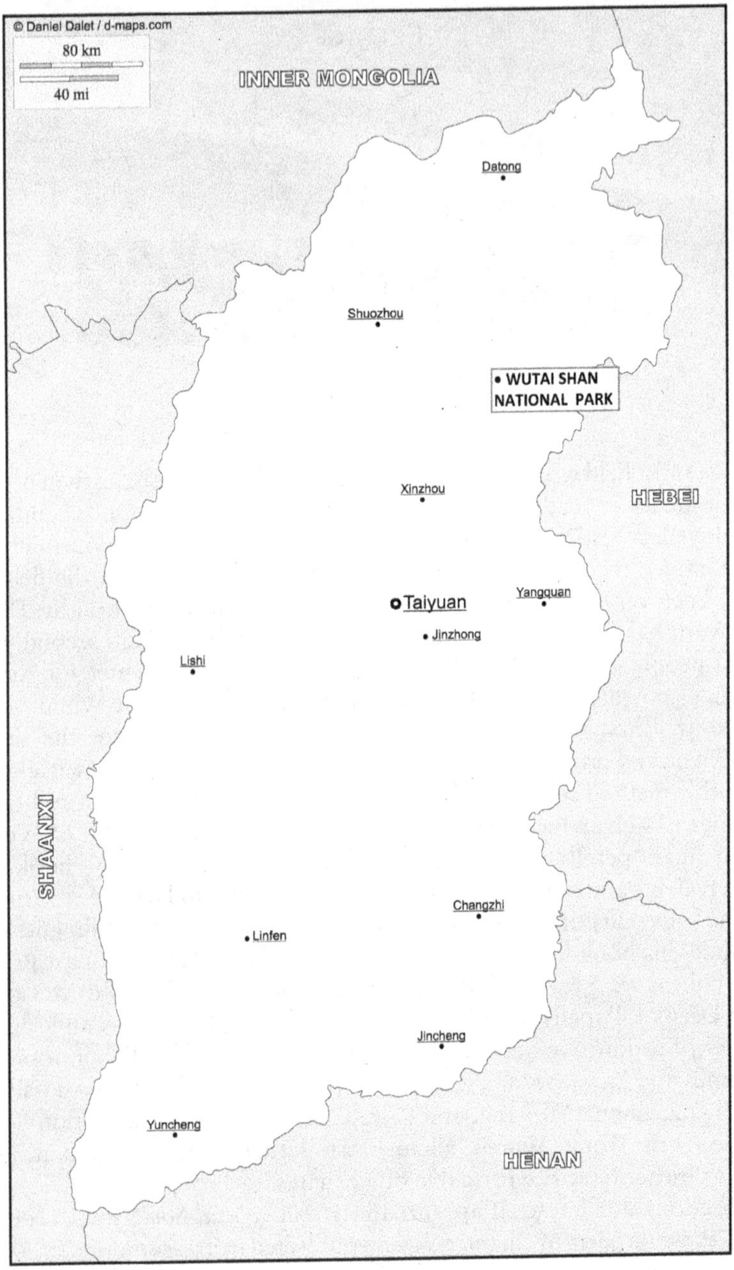

Shanxi Province, China, location of Mount Wutai National Park. Image courtesy of d-maps.com, http://d-maps.com/carte.php?lib=shanxi_map&num_car=17768&lang=en

Introduction

In March 2008, an article on the displacement of local residents by a state-directed development project in China appeared in the *Manchester Guardian*, one of the United Kingdom's most prestigious dailies. A story about the forced removal of residents in the name of national development by China's authoritarian government was not in itself unusual. This is a commonly reported topic in the Chinese popular media and occasionally appears in North American and European media outlets, usually as evidence of state-sponsored or endorsed human rights abuses. What was unusual about this story was the location of this displacement, a small mountain valley in central Shanxi province, and the development project at hand, a world heritage site within a newly created national park. Mount Wutai, known in Chinese as *Wutai Shan*, is one of China's four sacred Buddhist mountains. Mount Wutai is not actually a single mountain but a valley surrounded by five (*wu*) peaks (*tai*), corresponding to north, south, east, west, and center. Initially a Daoist retreat, it was transformed into a Buddhist site in the fifth century AD when the rulers of the Northern Wei Dynasty ordered the construction of temples dedicated to the Bodhisattva Manjusri (*Wenshu*). Over the next fifteen centuries, Wutai became home to dozens of Tibetan, Mongolian, and Chinese monasteries, temples, nunneries, and auspicious natural sites such as caves and rock formations, a destination for Dalai Lamas and emperors, and a pilgrimage center for Buddhists through much of East Asia.

After the Chinese Communist Party (CCP) came to power in 1949, religious buildings at Wutai were initially protected by government authorities as historical sites while religious practice was discouraged.

Amid the chaos and violence of the Cultural Revolution (1966–1976), local residents by their own account prevented marauding Red Guards from looting and destroying most of these buildings. Nevertheless, religious practice was banned and temples and monasteries closed. Only in the last two decades has a measure of religious freedom returned. Although practices continue to be monitored and managed by state authorities, 47 monasteries are now opened, with more than 1,500 monks and 500 nuns in residence, making this the largest concentration of religious devotees in China outside Tibet.

After the Communist Party instituted economic reforms and a modicum of religious practice was allowed, provincial authorities, acting under Ministry of Culture guidelines, decided to market Wutai Shan as a tourist attraction to Westerners and Buddhists from surrounding countries such as Japan, Hong Kong, and Southeast Asia. Their intention was not to promote religious practice but to create a sustainable source of economic development for a relatively isolated and marginalized area. The State Council subsequently declared the Wutai valley a national scenic spot (*jingdian*) in 1982, a national forest preserve in 1992, and added it to China's tentative list of UNESCO heritage sites in 2001. After several years of negotiations between the Ministry of Culture and UNESCO authorities, Wutai was approved as a world heritage site in 2009. According to the preservation plan agreed to by Chinese authorities and their counterparts at ICOMOS (International Council on Monuments and Sites), commercial and residential areas in and around the town of Taihuai, location of most of the protected buildings, would be relocated to the southern boundaries of the new national park, twenty-three kilometers away. Their homes, shops, and farm land would be replaced by green space and park lands, designed to accentuate the importance of the temples and monasteries listed as heritage sites.

Although the location (a rural community, not a bustling urban neighborhood) and subject matter (a heritage site, not a shopping mall or apartment complex) is unusual in news accounts of forced removal, the *Manchester Guardian* article followed a predictable narrative in foreign news reports about China: "The State" forcibly removing powerless local residents who found themselves in the path of state plans for development (in this case, paradoxically, a plan aimed at preservation). Local residents were quoted as complaining bitterly of the low sums they were paid for their land and homes and the poor quality of the housing they were offered in a new settlement far away from Taihuai (Branigan 2008). The thesis of the story was quite clear: despite economic and social changes in the People's Republic of China, when The State desired to act, Society could only go along or be forcibly pushed aside. This narrative, applied to everything from the Internet, family planning, and mass media to urban development and the organization of the 2008 Olympics, is such a commonplace rhetorical device in news about China that it is easy to accept this as a foundational truth.

Yet in this case (as in many), actors in this drama are far more complex and far less monolithic than a state versus society formula suggests. In fact, it is difficult to define a cohesive state view in this project to turn a vibrant religious community into a world heritage site. Both horizontally and vertically, different sections and sectors within the Chinese state have had very different interests in the ongoing reworking of space at Wutai Shan. Government forestry and tourism officials, cultural preservationists, state security personal, economic development planners, and religious affairs bureaucrats not only do not share the same goals for this project but are also divided at the national, provincial, and local level. At the same time, society in this story about an out-of-the-way place that has become a world heritage site is difficult to identify in a singular sense. Without going to the libertarian extremes of Margaret Thatcher's boast that "society doesn't exist," one should also be hesitant to accept without question a claim of a monolithic public that shares a foundational set of interests. In this case, there is no homogeneous local opposition to the state. Residents who have been displaced and those who are in line to be displaced are divided over compensation rates, personal relationships to local authorities, and the question of who counts as local. And local religious personnel, far from opposing this government plan to radically transform the space of Wutai Shan and turn religious practice into a tourist attraction, appear to implicitly endorse this if not openly embrace it.

RELIGION, HERITAGE, AND TOURISM

This book is an analysis of a particular type of heritage preservation project, religious material culture sites that continue to attract practitioners. Unlike restored historical settlements such as the American colonial towns of New Castle, Delaware, or Williamsburg, Virginia, or political sites of preservation such as Independence Hall in Philadelphia or Mount Vernon, Virginia, a religious heritage site is simultaneously preserved and yet alive, caught between the preservationist ideal of freezing time and the practical realities of faith as a life practice. This tension is made more complex by the fact that the term "religious heritage site" is a social construct; "religion" as a universal category only takes on meaning when it is embedded in the particularities of specific practices, beliefs, and lived experiences. As a Buddhist religious site shared by Tibetan, Mongolian, and Han Chinese sects, Wutai Shan's religious realness is embedded in a set of grounded realities. First of all, it is a sacred geographic space, not a space that became sacred because it happened to have various sacred material sites. Second, it has never been frozen in time; its temples, worship halls, monasteries, nunneries, and related buildings have been built, rebuilt, renovated, improved upon, demolished, dismantled, and added to since it was first identified as a place possessing a sacred aura in the fifth century CE. This practice of renewal and change at Wutai Shan was halted only after the communist takeover in 1949 and subsequent repression of public religious practice. In other words, the socialist revolution that aimed to make China modern through the application of scientific rationalism is the cause of Wutai Shan appearing to be a "heritage" site of seemingly ancient buildings, "untouched" by development. In fact, this built space was constantly being worked upon, shaped, and manipulated until 1949, when a revolution that claimed to focus squarely on the future froze this site in the past.

My subject in this book is the relationship between the preservation of religious sites as heritage, the promotion of tourism as an economic development resource, and governance in China, using Wutai Shan as a case study. Research in English on sacred space and tourism has largely focused on European and American sites (cf. Nolan and Nolan 1992; Vukonic 1992; Bremer 2003, 2006) that are mainly Judeo-Christian destinations (Winter and Gasson 1996; Santos 2002; Shackley 2002). A key exception is Shackley (1999), who examined the interactions between European and American tourists and religious practitioners at Buddhists sites in Nepal. This study differs in that foreign tourists (used here as in Chinese to refer to Euro-Americans) are almost entirely absent at Wutai Shan. Instead, the overwhelmingly majority of the approximately two million annual visitors to Wutai Shan are Chinese citizens, primarily of the Han nationality. Taking advantage of increased personal autonomy, higher disposable incomes, and a relaxation in government and Communist Party control over religious practice, urban residents travel to Wutai Shan for on average two or three days where they visit temples and engage to some degree in religious practice. Rather than being an open air museum for the world to experience as part of a shared world heritage, Wutai Shan appears to be returning to the role it occupied in Han Chinese, Tibetan, and Mongolian society before the collapse of imperial rule in the years after the 1911 Revolution: a Buddhist destination that attracts common people; Tibetan, Mongolian, and Han devotees and pilgrims; and wandering monks.

Since the establishment of the People's Republic in 1949, Chinese state authorities and the Chinese Communist Party (CCP) have had a vexing relationship with China's material past, particularly religious sites. In the years immediately after 1949, state authorities restricted religious worship and nationalized most cultural sites but also funded preservation programs. Perhaps the most famous example of desacralized heritage space during this era was the transformation of Beijing's Forbidden City into an open-air museum and park for the public at large. During the Great Proletarian Cultural Revolution (1966–1976), Red Guards were encouraged by the Maoist faction of the CCP to destroy tangible cultural heritage as part of a campaign against the "Four Olds" (customs, habits, ideas, and culture). However, since economic reforms began in 1978 after the triumph of Deng Xiaoping's pragmatism against the hard-line ideology of his Maoist opponents, the Chinese government has invested significant resources into cultural preservation and has become a major supporter of the world heritage movement. To this end, various state entities have worked closely with UNESCO to achieve World Heritage status for important cultural heritage sites while actively encouraging the development of a domestic tourism industry focused in large part on "heritage" (*yichan*), a neologism that only appeared in Chinese political discourse in the last two decades.

Recent ethnographic studies of tourism and heritage issues in China include Nyíri (2006a), Notar (2006), Su and Teo (2009), and Xie (2010). However, Nyíri, Notar, and Su and Teo focus on tourism in minority areas—Nyíri among Tibetan residents in Sichuan, Notar among Bai residents of Dali in Yunnan, and Su and Teo on the hegemonic aspects of heritage tourism in the Naxi world heritage town of Lijiang, also in Yunnan. Xie analyzes issues of authenticity and culture among Chinese tourists on the resort island of Hainan and thus does not speak to issues of heritage preservation. Though the collection of case studies in Oakes and Sutton (2010) focuses on tourism and faith in China, none of these examines the heritage process at Wutai Shan. General anthropological studies of heritage and tourism projects are widespread. However, many of these are either highly theoretical (Oakes 1998; Minca and Oakes 2006) or not specific to the particularities of how tourism and heritage are conceptualized and enacted in China (Layton et al. 2001b; Timothy and Nyaupane 2009).

Tourism has grown dramatically in the last decade in both Asia in general and China in particular, driven not by foreign arrivals but by regional and domestic demand. As Tim Winter (2007) has argued, these changes raise new questions about the relationship between heritage preservation, tourism practices, and normative assumptions about tourist motivations. These developments also point to the different interests and desired outcomes among transnational institutions, domestic policy makers, and local citizens at a site such as Wutai. For example, UNESCO's Tourism Program emphasizes the development of sustainable tourism practices at world heritage sites while ICOMOS advocates the application of universal conservation principles while promoting cultural diversity (Brooks 2002). A key question to the latter approach is how supporting cultural diversity would not actually contradict the promotion of a particular set of conservation principles as universal.

This emphasis on protecting cultural diversity through the application of universal principles also raises questions about the extent to which Euro-American cultural assumptions about the relationship between culture and nature, the place of humans in nature, and the meanings embedded in and location of a distinct sphere called "the environment" are universal. Globalization as a process has meant the promotion of not just neoliberal market ideology and an individual human rights regime but also a very specific environmental consciousness, one which locates nature as elsewhere (Weller 2006:6). This separation of not just nature and culture but also civilization and the environment has yet to become fully universal as seen for example in ongoing debates about the balance between wildlife protection and human development in places ranging from Botswana to India. In China, an emphasis on the separation of human action from nature is at odds with both Confucian and Buddhism perspectives. In this regard, Wutai Shan serves as a case study for the underlying paradox of the cultural preservation movement: in an attempt to protect and maintain global cultural diversity in the face of a relentless globalization, this ideology presumes that diversity can be promoted by mandating a universal system of spatial organization, one which requires cultural and natural sites defined as preservation worthy to be separated from ongoing social action. The net result is not diversity but sameness, a universal spatial logic that separates culture and heritage from vague notions of the market and commerce, or to use the language of UNESCO, core zones surrounded by in turn buffer zones and commercial zones. The irony is that this policy requires systematic *destruction* (of existing communities in and around heritage sites), *construction* (of heritage facilities and buffer areas such as green spaces), and *resettlement* (of displaced residences to areas outside of heritage zones). What makes Wutai Shan unusual is that world heritage status has also stimulated what from a preservationist perspective is completely unexpected, the *reconstruction* of former temples and the construction of new religious buildings.

This reality also runs counter to planning intentions at the local level in China. As part of the radical reorganization of society that followed the collapse of Maoism and the political shift to market socialism, central government authorities have sharply decreased direct funding to provincial and subprovincial bureaucracies. This has left local officials scrambling to find new funding sources and is a major reason for the exponential growth of the cultural heritage and tourism industries since 1998. If after 1949 a strong central government actively aimed to redefine and revolutionize sacred spaces by re-marking these as "red" (revolutionary) destinations, local and provincial authorities now are actively seeking to redefine these same sites as economic-tourist resources, now called "cultural heritage" (Dott 2010:44–45). This is taking place as the Communist Party has attempted to shift its rationale for political control from ideology to what Lee Ching Kwan has argued is rule *by* law, not the rule of law (Lee 2007:10). Though Lee's analysis is of labor relations, her central thesis is applicable to my own argument about the intrastate tensions involved in heritage projects and associated displacement and compensation issues:

> In oversimplified terms, decentralization makes local government responsible for developing a pro-business local political economy, while the same local government agents are called on to implement labor laws [*and also compensation laws*] promulgated by the central government eager to resolve labor conflicts and to maintain social stability. This tension between accumulation and legitimation, between the interests of the local and the central government, gives rise to endemic violations of labor rights and entitlements. (Lee 2007:11)

This governance tension points to another conflict at this site. When traditional pilgrimage destinations such as Wutai Shan are reframed as not just heritage sites but in this case as a national park, practical management questions follow (Olson 2006). Who must pay to enter, and who is exempt? How to manage the impact of increased arrivals on both the tangible site(s) and the aesthetics of the experience? Moreover, heritage (preservation) potentially conflicts with tourism (development) but also with religious practice. The overwhelming majority of visitors to Wutai Shan are Chinese citizens with what appear to be religious intentions, which raises a new set of questions. Can a living religious site also function as a heritage site? To what extent is a world heritage site visited almost solely by domestic Buddhist practitioners for primarily religious reasons actually a world heritage site? Finally, is tourism actually a problem that must be restricted and controlled at this site, if the vast majority of tourists, local residents, and monastic personal do not perceive this as a problem, or necessarily perceive visitors as simply tourists but instead as visitors with religious intentions?

China and the Party

One of the challenges in analyzing contemporary China is accurately describing the social, economic, and political realities of the PRC. Although nominally a "People's Republic" ruled by the Chinese Communist Party (CCP), there is precious little socialism remaining in practice, while finding a Party member who actually believes in communism is quite difficult. Indeed, on more than one occasion Chinese acquaintances have pointed out to me that the United States has more socialism in practice, in the form of welfare and unemployment benefits, Medicare, Medicaid, and Social Security, than does contemporary China. The CCP describes the current socioeconomic system as "socialism with Chinese characteristics." According to the official narrative, the Party has not repudiated communism but repositioned this as a future stage of development. This is not, of course, how the CCP ruled in its early years. During the first three decades of the Peoples Republic (1949–1979), the Party was dominated by Maoism, which explicitly assumed that universal stages of history described by Marx and shared to some extent by the current generation of modernization theory advocates could be transcended through extraordinary effort. Thus, Party Chairman Mao Zedong promoted first the Great Leap Forward (1958–1961), a political campaign aimed at rapidly transforming the largely agrarian economy into an industrial powerhouse within a few years, and then the Cultural Revolution (1966–1976), which was supposed to revitalize the revolutionary spirit of the CCP by eliminating a stagnant core of bureaucratic leadership while destroying the intangible and tangible basis of Chinese culture. The Great Leap Forward was disastrous, leading to massive food shortages and systematic violence that caused the deaths of almost thirty million people (Dikötter 2010). During the Cultural Revolution, hundreds of thousands of teachers, bureaucrats, party members, and everyday people were attacked, beaten, sometimes killed, and in a number of cases driven to suicide by youthful gangs of Red Guards, many of whom were subsequently resettled in rural areas beginning in 1968 as a means of restoring a semblance of political and social order.

The official Party narrative is that the Cultural Revolution was largely the work of the so-called Gang of Four, centered on Chairman Mao's wife Jiang Qing. After Mao's death, Deng Xiaoping purged Maoists from the leadership, promoted a policy of "Four Modernizations" (agriculture, industrial, scientific, and military), established Special Economic Zones (SEZ) along the east coast, and famously proclaimed that "to get rich is glorious." While victims of Mao's social experiments were rehabilitated (often posthumously), sent-down youth allowed to return to urban areas, and ideological Maoism abandoned, neither the government nor the Party has ever allowed an open discussion of the violence of the Sixties. One of the central ironies of contemporary China is that many of the bureaucrats and entrepreneurs who have accumulated private wealth in the decades since Deng's reform measures took effect and still hold power are from this generation of either formerly radicalized youth who had served as the foot soldiers of Mao's Cultural Revolution or its victims. Unlike in the United States, the Sixties does not evoke for many people in China summers of love or peace, but of chaos, violence, suffering, and ultimately disillusionment. This illustrates one of the most pressing social issues confronting the government: a widespread cynicism and lack of belief in most anything beyond accumulating wealth.

In contemporary China, a society in which doing business and getting rich is deemed to serve the nation, the Communist Party has abandoned socialism, and stability is the overriding political focus, religious practice and participation is generally tolerated. Religious practice is now seen as a potential source of social and ethical order (replacing Maoism and even communism) and a cultural resource that can serve the tourism industry (Oakes and Sutton 2010:10). In addition, although the Party may have abandoned Maoism it still officially accepts the evolutionary framework of Marxism. From this perspective, the eventual disappearance of religious belief and practice is taken as a scientific fact (Anagnost 1994:236). Thus, much as with state support of minority cultural practices, tolerating and even promoting selective current religious practices is deemed to not be a threat to Party rule because these beliefs will fade away in the future (Blum 2000).

However, the Party tolerates the practice of religion by private citizens within a particular set of boundaries. As long as religious practice is orthodox, practitioners, as well as religious orders, are largely left alone. Joining an officially registered monastery, enrolling in an official Christian or Catholic seminary, or studying in a state-funded Islamic school is no longer viewed as a threat. Indeed, religious practice is increasingly common as part of the shift in consciousness away from political thought work (*sixiang zhengzhi gongzuo*) to a widespread acceptance of following personal feelings (*genzhe ganjue zou*), whether in matters of sexuality (Farrer 2002) or faith (Yao 2007). According to government statistics, the total number of religious believers is 144 million, approximately 10 percent of the population. However the number is misleading because it accounts only for people who either have a formal affiliation or self-identify with religious institutions or associations of the five officially recognized faiths (Buddhism, Islam, Daoism, Protestant Christianity, and Catholicism). A much larger number of people engage in occasional religious practices without formal affiliation. In addition, folk practices (*minjian xinyang*) such as ancestor worship and lineage temples have been revived, particularly in rural areas, while fringe groups and various practices deemed superstitions (*mixin*) are closely watched, controlled, and usually suppressed (Yao 2007:173). This especially applies to activities labeled as superstitions and deemed to be feudal (*fengjian mixin*), which the CCP defines as any that involve a medium or formal social network, as opposed to common superstitions (*yiban mixin*), another term for folk practices.

Contrary to both Marxist theory and Party doctrine, the reform movement's success in broadly raising living standards has not led to a decline in religious practice. Instead, as personal incomes have risen along with increased individual agency, ritual practices have increased (Anagnost 1994). Both social science research and popular media reports suggest that a much broader part of the population practices religion to some extent, particularly Buddhism, than official statistics show (cf. Chau 2011). For example, the *Beijing News* reported that 65,000 people visited the city's Yonghegong Buddhist temple on February 3, 2011, the first day of the Lunar New Year, with hundreds of people having lined up as early as four in the morning to be first inside when the gates opened at seven o'clock (*"66,000 shimin"* 2011). Many people, the paper reported, sought general good fortunes for the New Year while others had more specific requests in mind, such as a high score for their son or daughter on the national university entrance examination. And, as I shall describe in this book, sacred mountain areas such as Wutai Shan annually attract millions of visitors.

Deeming events such as this as evidence of a religious revival, however, is debatable. To some extent, more people now practice religion simply because they can. Others seek a new belief system to replace the vacuum left by the Party repudiation of Maoism or to cope with rapid changes in everyday life brought about by large-scale modernization. However, pragmatic utilitarian reasons should not be overlooked (Yao 2007). Buddhism in particular is booming in China, but not, at least for most practitioners, as a vehicle for spiritual salvation or as an escape from materialism. Instead, it is increasingly viewed as a means of accentuating material gains, gaining or maintaining health, or achieving specific goals.

This is illustrated by the most common Chinese translation of the English word "worship," *bai*. Unlike the English term, however, *bai* is used specifically to describe acts of praying to Buddha (*baifo*, "worshipping or paying reverence to Buddha"), usually in the form of burning incense and ritually bowing. Praying in contrast to worshipping is usually associated with the Abrahamic religions in China and is translated as *qidao*, to entreat or beg. Thus, while all acts of piety at Buddhist temples are described as worshipping Buddha, the actual intentions of practitioners may not be what in English are usually perceived as the intentions of worship. Because of this ambiguity, in this book I shall not translate *baifo* but instead use this Chinese term to describe religious practices at Wutai Shan.

This illustrates a further ambiguity, the concept of religion itself in China. Despite centuries of presence within the country, Christianity and Islam are still widely considered to be foreign religions, while Buddhism, also a foreign import, is generally accepted as the normative faith.

The widespread use of religious sites as tourist and heritage destinations is a continuation of previous Party and State efforts to control religious practice. Both under Mao and during the ongoing reform period, major religious sites have not been destroyed. Other than at the height of Maoist radicalism, the Party did not advocate a deliberate policy of physical destruction of religious sites. Instead, temples, churches, and mosques were turned into schools, warehouses, and other public facilities, reflecting the utilitarian aspects of communism-in-practice. From the village level up through all layers of society, the Party-State appropriated religious space for educational and recreational purposes (Anagnost 1994). Until recently one could argue that state officials sought to cleanse these religious spaces of ritualized faith, defined in the language of the Party as feudal (*fengjian*) and superstitious (*mixin*), and transform them into healthy spaces (222). Yet an examination of the religious economy of Wutai Shan productively confuses this assumption and demonstrates quite the opposite. The State and Party no longer seek to eradicate faith by banning its practice and seizing control of sacred space. Instead, it now seeks to manage faith.

Book Outline

I begin with an analysis of cultural heritage as an ideological concept, the role of UNESCO and associated organizations in shaping this and the growth of a global heritage industry. In doing so, I discuss the emergence of a wilderness aesthetic in parts of Europe and North America in the mid-nineteenth century that was premised on a distinction between wilderness and civilization, a division that later served as the conceptual basis for both forest preservation and national park advocates, particularly in the United States. I am interested in unpacking the links between this familiar split of nature and culture and the contemporary heritage movement, which has taken this Enlightenment concept and reworked the relationship. Culture has been renamed as heritage, separated from civilization (identified with modernization) and joined with nature, turning civilization, in the form of material development, into the most serious threat to preservation. In Chapter II, I turn to contemporary China and the connections between tourism and heritage promotion, nationalism, and an ongoing state-directed moral campaign to shape behavior, cultivate what in Chinese is called a civilized (*wenming*) consciousness, and promote a modern sensibility. The contrast cannot be clearer: while world heritage advocates such as UNESCO and ICOMOS tend to view civilization, in the guise of modernization and economic development, as a threat to heritage preservation, the Chinese Communist Party has embraced heritage preservation as a tool of not just economic development and therefore modernization but for the *civilizing* of society.

Chapter III introduces Wutai Shan in an historical context, the meaning and place of sacred mountains (Buddhist and Daoist) in China, and the reasons why this particular mountain area became a pilgrimage destination for not just Mahayana Buddhists but also Tibetans and Mongolians. This chapter also provides a close reading of project documents related to the Wutai Shan world heritage zone. It analyzes planner aspirations as well as a UNESCO-driven emphasis on functional segregation and demonstrates that such a strict division between nature and culture had no counterpart in Chinese history or philosophy at least until the 1911 Revolution and arguably not until the height of Maoism between roughly 1957 and 1976. I end the chapter by suggesting that different parts of the Chinese state have different interests at this site, thus complicating reductionist notions of the State being contested by Society.

The final two chapters provide an ethnographic description and analysis of the dynamics of the heritage preservation process at Wutai Shan. Chapter IV examines the ongoing transformation of the Wutai area into a world heritage site as experienced by local residents including townspeople, monks, nuns, monastic authorities, and state officials. As with the complexities of how the State views this site, I seek to show that no homogeneous local perspective exists. Instead, rather than resisting the imposition of a heritage zone, different types of local actors maneuver with and against both each other and bureaucratic interests to achieve favorable outcomes. In Chapter V, I shift my attention to visitors, describing through qualitative fieldwork the types of people who travel to Wutai Shan. I argue that the majority of these visitors are domestic citizens with religious intentions. Rather than being yet another manifestation of Shangri-la (an idyllic site of other-worldly beings catered to by local peasants, absent material concerns), an idealized open air museum for all the world to experience (the UNESCO vision), or a toolkit for further civilizing work (the CCP view), this world heritage site is returning to the role it occupied in Chinese society before the collapse of central authority in the years after the 1911 Revolution. World heritage status has stimulated a reinvigoration of the aura associated with this sacred mountain. In this sense, Wutai Shan is an example of how rapid economic development and modernization not only spur the development of tourism but also the reinvigoration of traditional religious practices under the guise of tourism. Far from being in conflict, economic development and tourism in this case intersect with and support heritage and faith.

Chapter I

What Makes a Place "Heritage"?

Since ratification of the 1964 International Charter for the Conservation and Preservation of Monuments and Sites, more commonly known as the Venice Charter, "heritage" has been the subject of more than forty international and regional conventions. Though this accord limited heritage to archeological sites and monuments, the definition of this term has steadily expanded to include buildings, gardens, entire urban and rural spatial zones, natural sites such as mountains and valleys, and, most recently, intangible cultural practices (Ahmad 2006:294). In defining this wide variety of sites, objects, and practices as part of a shared *world* heritage, the United Nations Educational, Scientific, and Cultural Organization (UNESCO) provides guidelines for preservation efforts aimed at maintaining and fostering global cultural diversity.

Heritage preservation and the notion of "world heritage" as emblematic of a global community are by-products of the emergence of "globalization" as a transnational category for academics, policymakers, and state authorities. Having been produced by a post-WW II shift toward a transnational order, both heritage and various campaigns to preserve this are premised on the assumption that globalization directly threatens both the tangible cultural products of the past and the intangible cultural practices that remain in the present. The UNESCO list of World Heritage Sites, which now numbers 936 sites in 153 countries and territories, is the most well-known product of this campaign. Although UNESCO lacks enforcement power to preserve and protect sites, a wide range of governments cooperate with it to identify, classify, and preserve examples of tangible world heritage. The aura of UNESCO status is sufficient to evoke international criticism and anger when heritage sites

---

are destroyed or threatened. For example, the looting of Iraq's National Museum after the occupation of Baghdad by American military forces in 2003 provoked international outrage, with UNESCO and the British Museum leading a consortium of museum professionals to protect what remained in the collection. Similarly, when Serb forces bombarded the Croatian city (and UNESCO heritage site) of Vukovar in 1992 and Taliban forces destroyed ancient Buddha statues at an undesignated site in Afghanistan's Bamiyan Valley in 2000, both incidents garnered widespread media attention in Europe and North America and have since come to symbolize transgressions against world heritage. And in both cases UNESCO has provided funding for restoration, citing these sites' global cultural importance (Šulc 2001:164; Baker 2008). Setting aside issues related to this quest to re-create these material sites, a set of fundamental questions remain: Whose heritage is being preserved and managed, by whom, for what purposes, and with what political implications?

Cultural heritage programs, such as national museums and monuments, are profoundly political activities, given that they seek to shape accepted narratives about the past for political purposes in the present. Rather than being simply straightforward attempts to preserve and remember one's own past, heritage projects have also functioned as a vital element in the larger project of modernization and consequently the appropriation of other people's pasts. But modernization is premised on a profound contradiction. Within this process, the past has simultaneously been portrayed as a repository of a collection of traditional practices to be overcome and as source materials for a state-directed and state-constructed story about the present in the service of the nation. This can be seen in, for example, the former Shah of Iran's promotion of Persepolis as the ancient birthplace of the modern Iranian state and the intense focus in Nazi Germany on documenting alleged cultural ties with Aryan India (Silverman and Ruggles 2007b:11). In these cases, a modernizing regime sought to assert links with an historical past to boost its own political legitimacy. But many more such examples exist, spanning the spectrum of political ideologies and geographic locations. In some cases, state authorities have highlighted the past to distinguish this from contemporary political realities. Thus for example, between 1898 and 1901, colonial authorities in Burma (the United Kingdom), Vietnam and Cambodia (France), and the East Indian archipelago (the Netherlands) established local archeological institutions to survey, document, map, and restore sacred sites. These included Angkor Wat in Cambodia, Borobudur on the island of Java, and Pagan in Burma (Anderson 2006:179). In each case, colonial authorities emphasized their benevolent role in the restoration of a (glorious) lost past, not as a model for the present, nor as a way to lay claim to cultural roots, but as a contrast to what they viewed as the degenerate status of their colonial subjects (181). In the postcolonial era, these same sites have served as symbols for starkly different regimes. Angkor Wat was displayed on the flag of the Kymer Rouge regime in Cambodia, while the New Order government of President Suharto in Indonesia used Borobudur as a symbolic marker of the ancient roots of Indonesia, despite the fact that contemporary Indonesia is a secular republic with an overwhelmingly Muslim population. Ironically, of these three Buddhist sites, only Pagan has not become a world heritage site, a situation which UNESCO authorities have raised repeatedly with the military regime that rules Myanmar.

Sacred sites are not the only type of material space to intersect with politics. For example, along with its ongoing economic modernization drive, Chinese authorities are conducting a national heritage campaign to create as much as to preserve the past. As part of this effort, authorities in dozens of Chinese cities have constructed historic "old towns" (*fanggu*, "copies of ancient places"), thematic neighborhoods built to resemble Ming or Qing Dynasty streets that suggest a utopian premodern China of small shops and street vendors (cf. Anagnost 1997:107). In the United States, similar old towns and festival marketplaces have become increasingly common since the 1980s (Shepherd 2008). These examples illustrate that cultural heritage is not synonymous with history; it is instead a selective and highly controlled process of portraying the past (Logan 2007:34).

Even in situations in which an ostensibly new approach is offered, as in the design and management of the Museum of the American Indian in Washington, D.C., politics is ever-present. In this case, the presence of what museum authorities term the "survivance" of indigenous groups in the contemporary Americas is celebrated while the violence done against these groups in the past is quietly ignored (Silverman and Ruggles 2007b:14).

Despite this ever-present political element, cultural heritage proponents often begin a discussion of this issue by asserting that what constitutes "heritage" and what role this plays in human action is widely agreed upon across political, cultural, and structural lines. Heritage, it is claimed, is "essential to personal and collective identity and necessary for self-respect" (Lowenthal 2005:81). It is presented as timeless, transcending both historical and cultural contexts, and the glue that ties peoples together:

> Heritage is our legacy from the past, what we live with today, and what we pass on to future generations. Our cultural and natural heritage are both irreplaceable sources of life and inspiration. Places as unique and diverse as the wilds of East Africa's Serengeti, the Pyramids of Egypt,

> the Great Barrier Reef in Australia and the Baroque cathedrals of Latin America make up our world's heritage. What makes the concept of World Heritage exceptional is its universal application. World Heritage sites belong to all the peoples of the world, irrespective of the territory on which they are located. (UNESCO 2008a)

If heritage belongs not to the communities, societies, or states in which specific sites are located but to all the peoples of the world, its maintenance and preservation logically are the responsibility of all as well. Following from this, it is logical to assume that the identification of and support for heritage sites is primarily a technical process aimed at preserving the most important material aspects of the past and the cultural diversity of contemporary societies from the dangers posed by market forces in an era of globalization. For example, Valery Patin of the International Council on Monuments and Sites (ICOMOS) has warned of "heritage supermarkets" filled with copies of "authentic heritage" (2002:138–139). Deciding what to preserve is a matter of using "objective and neutral scientific evidence to avoid the politicization of decision-making processes and to enhance compliance" (Maswoud 2000:357). Yet by foregrounding technical issues of preservation and management issues of conservation, UNESCO authorities and other supporters of world heritage downplay the political and social impact heritage projects have on local residents. In this sense, this project bears a strong resemblance to the apolitical claims of so much done under the guise of "development." As James Ferguson (1994) demonstrates in his analysis of a Canadian-funded rural development project in Lesotho, perceived development needs often serve as an entry point for increased bureaucratic control in communities defined as development project targets. Rather than being unintended consequences or mere side effects that can be explained away by resorting to the good intentions of actors, these results are in actuality instrumental effects (1994:255). Yet development actors, whether multilateral, bilateral, or NGOs, invariably define themselves as *not* engaging in political acts. For Ferguson, what results is a process he calls the "anti-politics machine," in which the political basis of any development intervention is submerged beneath a universal discourse of modernization, progress and development, with the result that local voices are erased and agency suppressed. After all, who can be against "development" and progress? Carried to a logical extreme, this process might lead to the collapse of social structures, the growth of oppressive state institutions, or in the case of Rwanda, genocide (Uvin 1998). In most cases, however, the net result is more business as usual: a seemingly endless cycle of development projects carried out by outside actors who, although often acting with the best of intentions, replicate the logic of colonialism. With little focus on the depoliticizing effects of development interventions and a profound faith in universally applicable plans of action, development actors mainly succeed in facilitating increased bureaucratic intrusions into the everyday lives of targeted subjects, not necessarily in increasing state capabilities or in making life either qualitatively or quantitatively better for intended recipients. The net result is that, for many subjects of development, life today is no better, and in some cases actually worse than life was for their grandparents (cf. Englund 2006).

Of course, this does not mean there is some sort of conspiracy at work to keep people in poverty, whether in terms of development in general or heritage projects in particular. Far from it; institutions such as UNESCO, the World Bank, and the United Nations Development Program (not to mention the dozens of bilateral development organizations and countless nongovernment organizations involved with heritage) are staffed by people who undoubtedly do not aim to harm the disadvantaged and oppressed. Nor is it possible to say that all of these groups, working on a range of projects at multiple levels of engagement, do not understand history or are bad researchers, managers, or planners. Instead, as Ferguson notes, the point is to try to understand how particular perspectives come to be seen as normal, as "just the way things are" (Ferguson 1994:28; see also Elychar 2005:33). How does it become normal for people to accept as fact what, from any practical perspective, seems quite ambiguous, such as the claim that "legacies of both nature and culture belong not simply to their places and peoples of origin but to all the earth and its inhabitants" (Lowenthal 2005:85)? To give this claim context, what would it mean for citizens of, say, France, or Japan, or Fiji, to claim partial ownership over the Great Wall of China or Machu Picchu in Peru? In what sense does the Potala Palace in Lhasa "belong" to the world at large? More broadly, how and why has the preservation of certain material cultural sites, natural sites, and more recently, intangible cultural practices come to be accepted as not just desirable but a necessary duty of right-thinking international citizens?

Though interest in cultural heritage preservation initially focused on preserving tangible aspects of culture from the destructive impact of modernization and development, this project is increasingly viewed as a viable aspect of development. Indeed, rather than only protecting "culture" from the hegemonic power of "the market," cultural heritage programs are now increasingly linked to economic development, as a UNESCO Administrative Council member described:

> Long considered a luxury of the affluent, heritage has asserted itself, in the course of the past two decades, as a recognized component of development. From now on heritage will be taken into account when anyone reflects on new strategies of development. (Musitelli 2002:327)

Redefined as a cultural resource, heritage is now viewed much like other resources, as a product that can either be used up in the process of being exploited in the name of development or (productively) conserved under a form of stewardship. This transformation of culture into a resource that either is to be exploited for development or protected from the corroding effects of the market process mirrors environmentalist debates between preservationists, conservationists, and market proponents. This also has given UNESCO a central role as arbitrator of what counts as world heritage and global protector of this. Coincidentally or not, this reinvention of UNESCO as global custodian of culture has occurred in the wake of its near collapse in the 1980s and 1990s. Under the leadership of its then Director-General Amadou-Mahtar M'Bow (1974–1987), UNESCO was strongly criticized by United States and United Kingdom leaders for a perceived anti-European and anti-American stance and its support for a new world communications order. This conflict reached its apex after publication of the 1980 UNESCO Report, *Many Voices, One World*, more commonly known as the McBride Report after its chairman, Sean McBride. This report criticized the influence of an international media situated largely in Northern states and called for stronger national media development, a position that critics argued implicitly questioned freedom of the press. Critics also pointed to how UNESCO money was allocated; in the early 1980s, approximately 80 percent of UNESCO's staff was employed at its headquarters in Paris, and only 18 percent of its annual budget reached the field (Dutt 2002:33). The withdrawal of the United States from UNESCO in 1984 followed by the United Kingdom in 1985 resulted in a budget crisis, a revamping of the organization, and a scaling back of UNESCO activities. It also coincided with a new UNESCO focus on preserving global heritage through the application of a standardized planning model that emphasizes spatial segregation.

This planning vision is the product of a historically specific aesthetic perspective, High Modernist ideals of the mid-twentieth century that embraced functional segregation as a foundational organizational principle (cf. Scott 1998). But its roots go further back, to the late nineteenth century American wilderness movement led by figures such as the naturalist John Muir and city planner Frederick Law Olmstead, both of whom believed that physically separating contemporary built space from nature would ensure the preservation of the latter (Nash 1967; Graber, 1976). Muir, Olmstead, and their colleagues in turn drew on the insights of eighteenth century Romanticism, particularly the reimagining of mountains into sites to ponder in awe, not fear in terror (Nicolson 1959).

A Short History of Wilderness

For much of European history, wilderness, forests, and mountains have been foreboding places to avoid, the antithesis of a Biblical paradise (Nash 1967:8–9). Only with the popularization of Romanticism among newly emergent urban elites in the eighteenth century did an idealized untamed nature became a subject of contemplation. The Industrial Revolution, new forms of technology, and increased scientific knowledge about the world stimulated an aesthetic appreciation of the infinite, ironically as a reaction to the revolutionary transformation of material life that had created the conditions needed for a leisure class. The concept of infinity displaced the seventeenth-century assumption, born of an uneasy alliance between Biblical history and Cartesian logic, of a finite, mechanistic world destined to end (Nicolson 1959:160). In its place developed a foundational belief in the sublime, with nature as its subject. Lakes, valleys, forests, and mountains became (and remain) stages for what is supposed to be a personal experience with the awe-inspiring grasping of infinity, of nature-as-God and God-as-nature, seen in essays such as Emmanuel Kant's "Observations on the Feeling of the Beautiful and the Sublime" (1703), Edmund Burke's "A Philosophical Inquiry into the Origin of our Ideas of the Sublime and Beautiful" (1756), and Alfred Tennyson's "On Sublimity" (1826). Underlying this desire for the sublime was a primitivist suspicion of civilization as a corruptor of the soul (Nash 1967:470). This was reflected in sixteenth-century German literature that praised "wild man," British fiction such as Defoe's *Robinson Crusoe* (1719) that removed people from civilization, and Rousseau's idealized portrayal of the egalitarian *communitas* of Swiss village life in his *Social Contract* (1762).

The European settlement of the Americas began as a search for paradise but led to a confrontation with wilderness. In North America, the frontier ideal of independence and individualism constantly confronted the reality of physical threats from native peoples and animals, food and water shortages, and illness. It also grappled with a moral threat: the disappearance of civil standards as settlers move beyond settled lands (Nash 1967:25). Far from being a flight from civilization, the settlement of western lands in the United States was a centuries-long civilizing project, a taming and domestication of wilderness and nature. Writing in 1756, John Adams reflected this in his description of the New England colonies:

> Then the whole continent was one continued dismal wilderness, the haunt of wolves and bears and more savage men. Now the forests are removed, the bland covered with fields of corn, orchards bending with fruit, and the magnificent habitation of rational and civilized people. (quoted in Adams 1962:253)

By the mid-nineteenth century, the emphasis on conquering and settling wilderness lands to make them productive was being questioned. In 1832, George Caitlin (1796–1872), later famous for his portrait gallery of Native Americans, advocated the establishment of a national park that would showcase both animal and native life, "man and beast, in all the wild and freshness of their nature's beauty" (quoted in Nash 1967:101). In an *Atlantic Monthly* essay published in 1858, Henry David Thoreau suggested Congress establish "national preserves . . . in which the bear and the panther and some even of the hunter race, may still exist, and not be civilized off the face of the earth" (102).

Among Europeans, the roots of conservation were found in empires, not homelands, and focused initially on protecting wildlife from indigenous people for the benefit of colonial sport hunters. For example, German authorities established game preserves in their East African colony in 1896, and the first international conference on wildlife protection was held in London in 1900. In addition to calling for the banning of dynamite, nets, and poisons, delegates also suggested a restriction on native access to firearms as a way to protect potentially endangered species (Mackenzie 1988:205–207).

The life of John Muir (1838–1914) symbolizes the clash between the mystical and the practical, preservation and utilization, and contemplation and transformation. Widely revered as the father of the American environmental movement and the face of the Sierra Club, Muir was born in Scotland and grew up in rural Wisconsin. Despite lacking any formal education, he enrolled at the University of Wisconsin in 1860, where he studied botany, chemistry, and other sciences for three years before dropping out to learn from, in his own words, "the University of the Wilderness" (cited in Engberg and Wesling 1980:26). Influenced by Romantic poets such as William Wadsworth and John Ruskin, Muir spent the next decade wandering North America, supporting himself by working at different times as a sawyer, farm laborer, factory hand, machinist, and tour guide. Along the way he nearly was blinded in a factory incident in Indianapolis, spent a winter along Ontario's Georgian Bay, walked from Kentucky to the Gulf of Mexico, suffered from malaria in Florida, sailed to Cuba, crossed the Isthmus of Panama, and eventually reached San Francisco in 1868, which he left after one day for the Yosemite Valley. He then spent the next five years living in and around Yosemite, where he found his identity as a naturalist and environmentalist (9).

Yet despite his affinity for nature and his ceaseless campaign for its preservation, Muir had little interest in the people who actually lived in what he considered nature. Indeed, his written work contains almost no reference to the indigenous people he encountered in his travels. Instead, nature for him existed separate from civilization. In contrast to the dominant Social Darwinism of his time that firmly placed specific peoples at the center of a struggle to advance via the conquest of the natural world, Muir held a biocentric view of nature, one in which nature in effect became God (Wilkins 1995:265–266). Given this, Muir believed people could only be predators on nature or visitors to nature (Cohen 1984:190). From this perspective, natural spaces such as Yosemite should remain pristine and protected from the material world of civilization in order to serve as a respite from society. Writing in 1875, Muir argued that visits to such pristine natural places marked "the beginning of our return to nature, for going to the mountains is going home" (quoted in Cohen 1984:222). Yet he was also a harsh critic of tourists, believing they by and large did not know how to, or even care to, appreciate the splendors of places such as the Yosemite Valley.

Despite his contempt for tourism, by the late 1880s Muir had come to recognize that the preservation of sites such as Yosemite for their own sake was politically impossible. Instead, they had to be promoted to the public and Congress as tourist destinations. In other words, nature could either be preserved for tourism (which would enable and facilitate short-term visits) or exploited as a resource (by lumber mills, mineral companies, and shepherds). He therefore accepted the argument that those areas most worthy of protection and preservation possessed some sort of natural monument, such as unusual geological features. For example, the world's first National Park, Yellowstone in Wyoming and Montana, was described by its supporters in 1872 as a resource-poor area that nevertheless offered natural curiosities such as geysers. Moreover, it would be self-supporting through tourist revenue (Mason 2004:18).

To limit ecological damage, Muir also accepted the need to work with railroad companies to promote potential park lands in the American West as tourist destinations (Cohen 1984:203–206). Indeed, the establishment of Yosemite National Park in 1890 was supported by the Southern Pacific Railroad, which sought to create tourist destinations along its transcontinental route (Nash 1967:132).

This shift in Muir's approach raised a practical dilemma; how to champion nature as an antidote to society while being a critic of mass tourism? In other words, how to promote the value of preservation as "good for the soul" without having large numbers of everyday visitors transform preserved spaces into new outposts of civilization? Muir, as did Frederick Olmstead, argued that nature could only be fully grasped and experienced when a visitor was alienated from his or her own self as a result of life in civilization. Visitors who were not alienated were thus not to be encouraged.

He also accepted the need to collaborate with influential urbanites in Northern California. Founded in 1892 by a group of San Francisco professionals, the Sierra Club was initially a vacation club, with a charter that advocated for the preservation of mountain and forest areas not for spiritual reasons but instead egalitarian ones (Cohen 1984:281). It was also dominated by men with deep New England roots (Graber 1976:23–24). They promoted preservation as a public good based on the belief that public lands should be accessible to the public at large, not simply to commercial interests such as ranchers and timber barons or to spiritual wanderers such as Muir. This illustrates a split in the preservationist movement that continues to this today, reflected in tourist studies debates about the differences between "travelers" and "tourists" and use-rights disputes on public lands between environmentalists and recreationalists (26). One side views preservation as crucial for the soul and hence a solitary experience, the other views this as good for the body and therefore a communal experience.

The early preservation movement in the United States was based on a series of complex and at times contradictory impulses. For advocates such as Muir, preservation was a logical by-product of the Romantic tradition and crucial if people were to survive the alienating effects of industrialization. For others, such as Sierra Club members, preservation served a public good by providing natural playgrounds for vacationers. For nationalists, the creation of enormous national parks demonstrated the uniqueness of the United States vis-à-vis Europe. Finally, parks served a utilitarian purpose for railroads (by creating new destinations) and state governments (such as the case with the 1885 Adirondack Forest Preserve, which provided a stable water source for New York City) (Nash 1967:108).

These multiple reasons for preservation were contested in turn by conservationists, who argued for a stewardship model of land management. What links these different reasons was a shared assumption that the subject of these debates was in an untouched and hence natural state, devoid of human habitation. This of course was clearly not the case. For example, Shoshone, Nez Perce, and Blackfeet groups had inhabited the territory of what would become Yellowstone Park for centuries before the Park's establishment in 1870. When this territory became a National Park, these groups were considered a potential threat to tourists. But by the 1890s, with the founding of the Sierra Club, the creation of Yosemite Park in Northern California, and broader public support for preservation, indigenous groups across the American West had been transformed into a threat to nature itself (Mason 2004:25).

Despite evidence for the existence of human settlement in park lands, the American debate continues to focus on preservation (protection) versus conservation (management). Both sides in this debate take as self-evident the premise that parks do not have permanent inhabitants.

This perception is due in part because many American national parks were established on western lands that settlers had not appropriated[1] and also to how artists and writers framed and depicted park lands, their works becoming part of the popular imagination. For example, Ansel Adams, the most famous photographer of the American West in the early twentieth century, depicted national parks such as Yellowstone as resplendent sites of nature and hence art; rather than being simply parks, these were for him natural museums (Graber 1976:69). Yet missing from his images are people: it is as if these parks were cloistered from human civilization. But parks, like cultural heritage sites, require an audience. Without visitors, a destination literally cannot be a destination. The same assumptions hold true in other settler societies such as Canada and Australia. But in more historically grounded societies such as India and China, where continuous human settlement has existed for thousands of years, demarcating wilderness or untouched nature is difficult. This historical fact is complicated further by the cultural heritage movement, which has separated culture from civilization, equated the latter with the ills of modernity, and classified the former as part and parcel of nature and hence our collective heritage. Not just wilderness is to be protected from the ravages of economic development and modernization, as John Muir envisioned, but also the material culture of civilization itself.

UNESCO and Heritage

The first formal international attempt to regulate and protect nature was a conference held in Paris under the auspices of the League of Nations in 1933. Although never ratified, the final agreement from a follow-up conference in London called for the establishment of national parks that would adhere to a set of international management standards. In particular, this convention called for the regulation of settlements within park boundaries to protect animals and buffer zones of nature preserves around park boundaries (Mackenzie 1988:217).

As was the case with debates in the United States about land use versus land protection, this failed attempt at international standards focused on nature (in this case, wildlife), not culture. In the cultural realm, there was no movement for preservation, but instead for the promotion of universal cultural values. For example, the League of Nations Commission on Intellectual Cooperation, established in 1922, was tasked with promoting cultural tolerance and world peace (Dutt 2002:1–2). Later, in wartime London, the British government set up the British Council for Education in World Citizenship, with the goal of promoting international solidarity (Sewell 1975:35).

Upon its establishment on November 1, 1945, UNESCO was tasked by the United Nations with promoting world peace and security. The new organization initially addressed political, racial, and religious differences within and between societies with a secular humanist worldview based on an evolutionary framework. Although UNESCO now emphasizes the "C" (cultural) in its name, the organization originally emphasized the educational and scientific aspects of its mission. This is illustrated by the appointment of Julian Huxley, a prominent biological evolutionist and proponent of eugenics, as its first director. In 1947, Huxley authored a pamphlet aimed at a skeptical American audience in which he explained the purpose of the new organization. In this pamphlet, Huxley argued that human values were biological, not cultural, and advocated for the development of a universal philosophy to serve what he called the "spiritual and mental aspects of existence" (Huxley 1947:7–8). This could be done, he suggested, by first codifying "a unified pool of tradition for the human species as a whole" that could subsequently be provided to inhabitants of "backwards sectors" (17).

Building on this utopian vision, the 1964 Venice Charter called for an international framework for the preservation and restoration of ancient monuments because, in its words, "people are becoming more and more conscious of the unity of human values and regard ancient monuments as a common heritage" (ICOMOS 2003). The Charter, drafted by a twenty-three person committee consisting of nineteen Europeans, one Mexican, one Peruvian, one Tunisian, and one Asian (a Japanese representative from UNESCO), emphasized a technical and archeological perspective. It called for *in situ* preservation (Article 7), strict adherence to original materials (Article 9), and "special care" of sites "in order to safeguard their integrity and ensure they are cleared and presented in a timely manner" (Article 14). Noticeably missing from the Venice Charter is any recognition of communities living on or near monuments or sites.

The following year the Johnson Administration organized a White House conference at which a world heritage trust was proposed. This organization would identify and protect the world's most important cultural sites for the benefit of current and future members of the "international citizenry" (quoted in Slatyer 1983:138). A declaration issued at UNESCO's annual conference in 1965 recognized links between heritage sites and tourism development, while the 1966 general conference issued a statement calling for cooperation with the United Nations Development Program (UNDP) to develop cultural tourism (Sewell 1975:255). However, by the late 1960s, cultural preservationists and others, primarily in the developed world, voiced new concerns about the threat both tourism and economic development posed to cultural sites.

Subsequently, UNESCO established a working committee to examine this issue in 1970, which lead to the 1972 World Heritage Convention. The World Heritage Convention defines world cultural heritage as any site, building, or monument that has "outstanding universal value" (Article 1). Damage to any item that qualifies as part of the world's cultural heritage is said to harm the heritage of all nations. Thus preservation is crucial. What qualifies for preservation and protection is to be determined by scientific, economic, and technical studies (Article 24). The Convention established a World Heritage Committee (WHC), consisting of twenty-one member states elected for two-year terms, to vote on applications for world heritage status. The actual evaluative process divides nominations into "culture" and "nature" and tasks the International Council on Monuments and Sites (ICOMOS) and the International Union for Conservation of Nature and Natural Resources (IUCN), respectively, to conduct evaluations. ICOMOS and IUCN in turn use a list of ten criteria, six "cultural" and four "natural," to examine potential sites for inclusion. Under WHC guidelines, potential sites must meet at least one of these criteria (UNESCO 1972:1).

The criteria are so broad and general, however, that it is reasonable to wonder what might not qualify. For example, what scientific criteria can actually determine "outstanding universal value" (Cleere 2001:23)? Under Convention guidelines, a cultural site or object can qualify if it is a "masterpiece of human genius" (i), "a unique or at least exceptional testimony" to a disappearing tradition (iii), an "outstanding example" of an architectural style (iv), or of a "traditional human settlement" (v), or represents "an important change in human values" (ii).

Despite these ambiguities, continual concern about the potential contradictions between economic development programs and cultural preservation, particularly among European member delegations, led to the publication of *Our Creative Diversity* (1995), the core UNESCO policy document on cultural heritage that prevails today. This report asserts that not only heritage sites but also cultural practices must be preserved because any loss to the world's diverse body of material culture harms the world's "reservoir of knowledge" (UNESCO 1995:179–181).

Diversity, however, is not what this report actually emphasizes. Instead, it advocates for a particular set of cultural values, precisely those which Julian Huxley so passionately argued for in 1947. *Our Creative Diversity* defines culture as a world view based on tolerance, pluralism, and most importantly an acceptance of a "global ethics" of equality, democracy, and human rights (UNESCO 1995:15–16). Yet, while harshly critical of what it terms an "all-pervasive" homogenization of culture (16), this report ignores the fact that the values it seeks to preserve are arguably not global values at all but instead a particular set of values embedded in the culture of secular humanism. Rather than a manifesto in the name of diversity, *Our Creative Diversity* is in fact a manifesto for a global order based on a very specific set of cultural values.

For example, while asserting the right to culture, the authors of *Our Creative Diversity* also assert that "universalism is the fundamental principle of a global ethics" (UNESCO 1995:46). This claim of a universal ethical framework not only raises questions about what constitutes a UNESCO-approved form of cultural pluralism, but also points to two related issues, the origins of such a framework and the contradiction between a universal value system and the social realities of actually existing communities. This position echoes a division of (local) culture and (global) civilization. This split, rooted in German Romanticism, defines culture as the sphere of the local, intuitive, and experiential and civilization as that of the cognitive, rational, and universal (Eriksen 2001:137). Reason is taken to be universal, while culture is taken to be particular, the net result being a problematic encounter between the truth claims of any universal position and the subjective perspectives of local social realities and political positions.

UNESCO authorities recognize that cultural and natural heritage can also be simultaneously viewed (e.g., by its sister organization UNDP) as cultural and natural *resources*. Thus *Our Cultural Diversity* states that each society must "assess the nature and precariousness of its heritage resources on its own terms" to decide what uses to make of them in "the spirit of development" (UNESCO 1995:176) while guarding against allowing cultural heritage to be transformed into a "tourist resource" (184). Underlying this unease with tourism is an assumption that cultural products and heritage sites must be protected from market forces that might encourage the commodification of both tangible and intangible cultural forms.

This assumption that people are a problem when it comes to the protection of heritage is evident in the official *Nomination Report for Mount Wutai*, which cites unregulated tourism and local residents as the primary threats to the preservation of Wutai Shan:

> The largest threats to the physical conditions of the temples and ancient buildings lie with unauthorized constructions of tourist service facilities in the surrounding area of the Taihuai Proposed Core Zone, which have seriously marred the historical and environmental integrity as well as the religious ambience. (GOC 2008b, 228)

To address this threat, plans call for the relocation of most residents of Taihuai to a new satellite community situated outside the park's south gate (GOC 2008a:185), thus replicating a UNESCO emphasis on functional and spatial segregation at world heritage sites. UNESCO conceives of a heritage site as a series of zones, ranging from a culturally pristine core to an impure outer zone of commerce and local life. This is made clear in UNESCO's most recent operational guidelines for world heritage sites, which stipulate that clearly delineated boundaries and a buffer zone must be established at each site by state authorities to protect it from "human encroachments" (UNESCO 2008b:26). This demarcation of space is promoted by UNESCO as a universal principle of preservation, despite its own claimed emphasis on cultural diversity. Indeed, UNESCO planning guidelines assert that a site holds universal value only if its cultural values are "truthfully and credibly expressed" through factors such as form, function, setting, and materiality (22). Furthermore, a site can only be evaluated "within the cultural contexts to which it belongs" (21). This illustrates the central role that archeological principles of excavation and presentation have had in how heritage has been conceptualized beginning with the Venice Charter. Because the Venice Charter's focus was on the conservation and restoration of historic monuments, an emphasis on *in situ* principles to preserve the archeological record was quite logical. However, since 1964, the scope of tangible heritage protection has been extended far beyond ancient monuments to include entire neighborhoods, communities, and, in the case of areas such as Wutai Shan, valleys filled with worship sites. Despite this expansion of the subject matter of heritage protection, tangible heritage continues to be defined primarily in archeological terms, which resituates any type of material culture defined as heritage into an archeological site, and hence primarily important because of its links with the past, not the present. This fossilization of heritage at living heritage sites such as Wutai Shan is particularly problematic precisely because they are not museum sites. Moreover, evaluating such sites "within the cultural contexts" to which they belong necessitates an acceptance of mixed space use at Buddhist religious sites such as Wutai Shan. This is because these are heritage sites at which commerce and faith, the sacred and the profane, and tourism and religion have been bound together for centuries.

Preservation as a Global Goal

In 1962, the first World Conference on National Parks was held in Seattle, Washington. Attended by representatives from sixty-three states, the final report of this conference emphasized preservation, recreation, and wildlife protection (Mason 2004:74–75). Delegates recommended that the International Union for Conservation of Nature (IUCN) draw up a list of critical areas to preserve and an international commission on park planning be established. They also suggested that donor countries make aid to newly established governments contingent on conservation and park development efforts (Adams 1962:380). Finally, they noted their concern with the threat an expanding world population posed to nature. Some speakers proposed a system of spatial segregation to protect critical areas from people. For example, Enrique Beltràn, a delegate from Mexico, suggested nature preserves be separated into three zones: a "general relaxation" zone for tourists, an "intermediate zone" that would have no facilities, and a core restricted zone that would be accessible only to the scientific community (Beltràn in Adams 1962:39).

This conference was followed in 1964 by the passage of the American Wilderness Act (PL 85-577) by the U.S. Congress. This law mandated federal protection of designated lands devoid of permanent human habitation, defining these as sites where "the earth and the community of life are untrammeled by man, where man himself is a visitor who does not remain" (quoted in Nash 1967:5). This law codified a geo-pious perspective on wilderness as a space for humans to visit to transcend the ordinary, experience the vastness of nature, and encounter a mythical Eden, or the world before humanity (Graber 1976:11). Of course, such a goal ignores the enormous human effort that is required to make nature look natural, from trail construction and soil erosion projects to the construction of sanitation systems and the management of forests.

Nevertheless, the underlying premise of this law has become a hegemonic model throughout the world. As with heritage itself, a shared set of assumptions about the environment based on what is supposed to be the proper relationship between "man" and "nature" link divergent state and nonstate actors. Facilitated by a transnational bureaucratic system centered on the United Nations and organizations such as Greenpeace, a particular discourse of environmentalism, centered on a suspicion of civilization, has come to seem second nature to many (Meyer et al. 1997:627–632). In its extreme form, this rejects even the parks movement as a debased form of "faking" nature, since this involves human intervention into an environmental space already tainted by human action (Elliot 1995). Yet the broader (and more mainstream) environmentalist discourse also insists that humans are part of nature, which implicitly renders an emphasis on wilderness preservation illogical (Sober 1995:234).

Tourism, as is often noted, is now the world's largest industry. But within this sector wilderness and nature are extremely lucrative subindustries. Commercial products such as camping equipment, outdoor clothing, off-road vehicles, and adventure travel tours all contribute to a new form of identity, that of the cosmopolitan naturalist. Members of a transnational class of like-minded consumers, cosmopolitan naturalists shop at one-stop outdoor stores such as REI and Sports Authority in the

United States and Decathlon in France, buy brands such as Nike, Gore, and North Face, and have the disposable income to ski in the Rockies or trek in the Himalayas. They do not hunt, or travel in groups (except with each other), and strenuously avoid indentifying as tourists. They also belong to organizations such as the Sierra Club and Greenpeace, support universal concepts such as human rights, and generally do not live in nature but instead in urban enclaves. They are, in short, the ideal subjects of UNESCO's metanarrative of a world community of heritage and culture. Yet they also personify the class basis of transnational campaigns for heritage preservation. The privileged beneficiaries of neoliberal globalization, cosmopolitan naturalists cultivate a wilderness ethic that rejects economic development. This conservationist ethic is in fact a paradoxical form of ecoconservatism, assuming that some peoples in specific places should be content to live "closer to nature." Yet what is good for nature is not always what is "good for humans" (Sagoff 1995:167). This concept is illustrated by the puzzling absence of culturally based views of humans and nature in debates within the growing field of environmental philosophy. Instead, actors are imagined to be idealized generic human subjects who exist and comingle outside the defining structures of culture (cf. Rolston 2003; Norton 2003; Elliot 1995). While some recognize that a culture of nature exists (Light 2003a), they fail to grapple with the fact that "nature" is conceptualized differently in different cultural environments.

The UNESCO concept of world heritage rests on the grandest of grand narratives, one that postulates a world of universal aesthetics that define a unified body of culture which in turn supposedly belongs to all people, everywhere. In this sense, it is a global *civilizing* project, one remarkably similar to the global human rights and environmentalism movements. Each of these campaigns assumes as fact a conventional fiction, a global community of secular humanitarians that transcends the nation-state yet draws its authority from nation-states. This perspective in turn is based on a postmodernist selective amnesia that erases actually existing social, political, and economic realities. In this sense, far from being polar opposites, the modernist Hegelian idealism of the world heritage movement (the world is one) and the neoliberalism of the postmodern view of history and politics (we are the world) supplement each other. By defining sites such as Wutai Shan as part of the *world's* heritage, existing social and political realities are ignored, replaced by a faith that imagines such places as repositories of world culture, to which all people everywhere have a claim.

The reality of course is that very few people in the world have the ability to visit and experience most world heritage sites. After all, it costs thousands of dollars for a European, North or South American, or

African to travel to China. For world heritage sites in materially affluent countries, the myth of world heritage is made even more apparent when applying for a visa. I very much doubt whether the American Embassy in Beijing, for example, routinely issues visas to Chinese citizens who explain it is their right as a member of the world community to visit the Liberty Bell in Philadelphia or Taos Pueblo in New Mexico.

Conclusion

The American national park movement sought to protect wilderness lands from human development and hence civilization. The voices of this movement have included naturalists such as John Muir and nature writers such as Edward Abbey and Aldo Leopold, all of whom shared a language of romantic primitivism with Romantic poets such as John Ruskin (Graber 1976:36–39). Over the course of the last four decades, this world view has been transformed into a transnational model that aims to protect both nature and culture, collectively defined as heritage, from civilization, now renamed as development. Given this, abstract debates about the proper balance between tourism and preservation, the preservation of nature and culture, and the degrading effects of development are of little relevance precisely because these are debates about how social realities should be, not how they are. This is because environmental and cultural realities, not just economic development realities, differ.

In the context of heritage preservation, a paradox is thus evident: in an attempt to preserve cultural diversity in an era of globalization, UNESCO officials promote a reorganization of local space at world heritage sites that erases culturally embedded place. In other words, to qualify for world heritage status, sites such as Wutai Shan must be radically reordered on the ground so that people and commerce are removed from a central zone of cultural preservation, thus replicating the logic behind the global conservation movement.

But the most paradoxical issue is that of responsible parties. Like UNESCO itself, heritage conventions and declarations are agreements between nation-states, not communities. Moreover, nominations for world heritage status can only be made through national governments (Cleere 2001:24). Subsequently, UNESCO authorities do not define the nomination process and management of sites as a joint project of local and national interests, let alone those of actually existing communities. Instead, the role of national authorities in the promotion and definition of heritage sites is framed as technical: state support of heritage preservation is taken as a good, in and of itself, thus ignoring the political questions of why certain state authorities seek world heritage status for particular sites and what impact these projects have on local communities and the people who inhabit these places.

The social fact that heritage landscapes are seldom simply landscapes but are invariably lifescapes, which supporters of heritage development projects often ignore or gloss over. This is done by first, defining preservation as a universal priority; second, by asserting that heritage projects will create local jobs, with little discussion of what type of jobs this might mean; and finally, by claiming that local residents gain a special status when their community is remade as a heritage site (Hackenberg 2002:294). The actual impact that heritage status has on local communities is of little import in these debates. Instead, the most common criticism among heritage project supporters tends to be UNESCO's lack of enforcement powers. For example, frustration is sometimes shown when states fail to follow through on their site nominations (cf. Maswoud 2000:360). This frustration is based on the assumption that states are always unified bodies and act in one interest, a position that has repeatedly been shown to be open to question in recent studies of development projects (cf. Elyachar 2005; Zhang 2004). This also assumes state actors act in the interest of local residents at proposed heritage sites.

Neither of these assumptions is necessarily valid in the case of heritage promotion in the People's Republic of China. Not only do different parts of the bureaucratic machinery of governance have different interests when it comes to heritage projects, but local residents at heritage sites such as Wutai Shan do not share the same goals and desired outcomes. Moreover, the underlying intention of UNESCO-sponsored cultural heritage projects (the strict preservation of sites as part of a *world* heritage) is at odds with the primary purpose of these projects at the national level in China: the cultivation of a common cultural moral code as a means toward improving the overall moral and spiritual quality of its subjects, not as world citizens but as modern Chinese.

It is this project I turn to in Chapter II.

Chapter II

Tourism, Heritage, and Moral Education in China

Jinbu wenming, tiechu fangbian
Improving civilization creates a better society
(Notice posted above urinals in a highway restroom, Shijiazhuang-Beijing Expressway, June 2011.)

One of the most reviled characters in the nearly century-old clash between shaping the present and maintaining the past is the quintessential tourist. The tourist, or so it is often claimed, has commercialized the cultural, degraded the priceless, and, in sheer numbers, caused irreparable harm to the material basis of our collective cultural heritage, all on a endless quest for authenticity. That such a naïve desire for the authentic can never be fulfilled has not stopped this tourist quest (MacCannell 1976). As noted in Chapter I, the perceived dangers of tourism and commercialization are an ever-present backdrop to discussions about preservation, especially within UNESCO.

As with discussions about the ethics of natural preservation, debates about the tourist threat to cultural heritage often assume an ideal subject, a stereotypical, middle-class, white European or North American who tours in predictable ways and for predictable reasons. This typecast and universalized tourist is the implicit Other to a cosmopolitan traveler. In place of cosmopolitan curiosity, action, reflection, and insight is, or so it is alleged, passivity, reaction, and a complete lack of knowledge about those who are toured. Tourists consume; travelers learn. Tourists distort the local, travelers become part of it. This fundamental class division has been a part of the European and North American travel

---

Faith in Heritage: Displacement, Development, and Religious Tourism in Contemporary China by Robert J. Shepherd, 43–68

canon for more than a century, and, as can be seen by the popularity of guidebooks such as the *Lonely Planet* series that promise their users an experience beyond what a tourist might ever gain, shows no signs of abating (Shepherd 2002).

Yet the case of China complicates this binary division of travelers and tourists as well as the death of culture at the hands of the market. One side effect of the rapid transformation of the Chinese economy from socialist planning to neoliberalism has been an explosion in the growth of both domestic tourism and heritage-related industries. Between 1980 and 2000, the number of museums in the PRC increased from 365 to 1,353 (Denton 2005:566). By 2005, this number had reached 2,200 and as of 2011 had passed 3,000. In May 2011, the National Museum reopened in Beijing's Tiananmen Square after a four-year, $367 million renovation that made this the largest museum in the world. In terms of tourism, 1.6 billion annual domestic tourist trips were made on average between 2007 and 2009, twice as many as in 1998 (CNTO 2007, 2009). The size and scope of Chinese domestic tourism now overshadows annual international tourism arrivals, which as of 2009 numbered approximately 130 million. Although this sounds considerable, the number is misleading because the majority of foreign tourists are ethnic Chinese residents of Hong Kong, Taiwan, and Macau. For example, in 2009, the actual number of non-Chinese arrivals totaled just 21.93 million, almost half of whom (10.2 million) were citizens of Japan, Russia, or the Republic of Korea, while only 7.1 million visitors were from Europe and North America (CNTO 2008, 2009). As these statistics illustrate, the tourism industry in China is overwhelmingly domestic and regional, and the impact, whether economic or cultural, of arrivals from Western countries is minimal.

A different type of cultural space—folk, ethnic, and historical theme parks—has also expanded rapidly in the last two decades and now number more than 2,500. This industry began with the opening in 1989 of the "Splendid China" theme park (*Jinxiu Zhonghua*) near Shenzhen, in the heart of China's modernization drive in Guangdong Province. This was followed in 1991 with the opening of the first "China Folk Culture Village" (*Minzu Wenhua Cun*) nearby (Oakes 1998:49–50). This park displays building styles of twenty-three different minority groups, ranging from a Uighur Mosque and Tibetan Monastery to Mongolian Yurts and Dong bell towers (Sofield and Li 1998:382–383). Like Disney's Epcot Center in Orlando, Florida, the park's "inhabitants" are all "authentic" minority peoples. This park, like similar folk parks throughout China, is designed for and visited by mainly domestic tourists (Nyíri 2006a:15).

"Heritage" as a category is, paradoxically, a new concept in China, reflected by the fact that state officials created a neologism (*yichan*) only in 1982 to describe it. However, the scientific study of material culture began during the years of the Republic (1911–1949). The country's first archaeological research institute was established at Beijing University in 1925, and the first legal regulations on cultural objects were issued in 1930 (Murphy 1994; Zhuang, 1989). This was followed in 1931 by the "Statute for the Preservation of Scenic Spots, Points of Historical Importance, and Articles of Historical, Cultural, and Artistic Value" (Gruber 2007:272). The first formal attempt to categorize China's material heritage occurred in 1948, shortly before the collapse of the Nationalist government, when professors at Qinghua University in Beijing published a list of 450 sites under the title of *A Brief List of Important Architectural Sites in China*.

Following the establishment of the People's Republic of China in 1949, the new authorities sought to reshape history, particularly in urban areas, through the selective destruction of cultural sites and their replacement with new symbols of state power. For example, Beijing's city walls were torn down during construction of the city's first subway line between 1965 and 1969, and historic areas to the south of the Forbidden City were demolished in 1958–1959 during the construction of the Great Hall of the People and the expansion of Tiananmen Square. However, state authorities also preserved selected historic sites as examples of prerevolutionary feudalism. Thus in Lhasa, capital of Tibet, the Dalai Lama's former summer palace (Norbulinka) was opened to the public as a museum dedicated to his supposedly extravagant lifestyle shortly after he went into exile in 1959, while the house on Gulangyu island near Xiamen, Fujian Province, where Nationalist leader Chiang Kaishek stayed the night before he fled China in 1949, was maintained as a symbol of the defeat of the old regime.

Although the State Council issued a decree in May 1950 that called for the surveying and codification of historical sites, artifacts, and endangered animals, the first national regulations on cultural property were not issued until November 1961 (Zhuang 1989:104). This decree created the category of "National Cultural Relic Protection Units" (*Zhongdian Wenwu Baohu Danwei*), listed 180 such sites, and provided funding for restoration and preservation. These listed sites were divided into two categories, "ancient," such as tombs, grottoes, buildings, and stone carvings that predated the collapse of Qing authority, and "revolutionary" historical sites that commemorated Communist Party events and personages (Liu 1983:97).

This initial attempt to create a national cultural heritage system was disrupted by the outbreak of the Cultural Revolution (1966–1976), during which Communist Party Chairman Mao Zedong encouraged youthful Red Guards to destroy the "Four Olds" (customs, culture, habits, and ideas). During this decade of upheaval, thousands of historic sites including temples, churches, mosques, and other buildings were looted, desecrated, and turned into warehouses and other public buildings.

After a modicum of political stability was restored following the resettlement of radicalized youths in rural areas, the central government established the State Administrative Bureau of Cultural Relics and Archeological Data in 1973. But not until after Chairman Mao's death in 1976 and the return to power of pragmatists associated with Deng Xiaoping was cultural heritage legally codified, in the 1982 *Law on the Protection of Cultural Heritage of the People's Republic of China.* This law provided a new term for material culture, replacing "relic" with the neologism "heritage" (*yichan*); established guidelines for categorizing, excavating, and site protection; and expanded the number of listed "cultural relics protection units" to 242.[1] The purpose of heritage protection was to increase scientific research, support patriotism and revolution, and promote socialist culture (Zhuang 1989:105). The 1982 law, which remains the basis of state heritage policies, explicitly links heritage preservation with the political objectives of nationalism, socialism, and modernization (Sofield and Li 1998:370–371). In other words, preserving the past is not an end in itself. Preservation is instead supposed to contribute to the development of a national consciousness, reflect socialist values, and contribute to economic development and modernization.

Three years later, in January 1985, the Chinese government signed the *Convention on the Protection of World Cultural and Natural Heritage.* The potential contradiction between a state policy that defined heritage in political and economic terms and UNESCO's emphasis on a collective global heritage that transcended state boundaries was easily reconciled by Article Four of this Convention, which explicitly recognized that "the duty of ensuring the identification, protection, conservation, presentation and transmission to future generations of the cultural and natural heritage referred to in Articles 1 and 2 and situated on its territory, *belongs primarily to that State*" (UNESCO 1972, emphasis added). Moreover, heritage could even be reconciled with Maoism, by defining what should be preserved in the words of the Chairman himself: "Make the past serve the present and foreign things serve China" (quoted in Liu 1983:21).

As of 2012, China had forty-three UNESCO-designated World Heritage sites, fifty-two additional sites awaiting approval, and approximately twelve hundred heritage-related sites classified as "key cultural relic protection units." All of these sites fall under the loose domain of the State Administration of Cultural Heritage (SACH), known until 2003 as the "State Cultural Relics Bureau" (*Guojia Wenwu Chu*). China's world heritage sites include twenty-nine built heritage sites such as the Forbidden City, Temple of Heaven, and Summer Palace in Beijing; eight natural sites such as the Wulong Panda Reserve and Jiuzhaigou Valley in Sichuan Province; and four cultural sites situated in natural areas, all of which are mountain pilgrimage destinations. These four "mixed" destinations are Mount Tai (Taishan) in Shandong, Mount Emei (Emeishan) in Sichuan, Yellow Mountain (Huangshan) in Anhui, and Mount Wuyi (Wuyi Shan) in Fujian. Wutai Shan, although a sacred mountain area, is classified as a cultural site.

Below the national level, the total number of officially designated and potential heritage sites is staggering. Already by 1989, there were approximately 3,000 provincial-level sites and more than 10,000 county- and city-level sites, and a 1981 government survey identified approximately 100,000 total potential sites (Zhuang 1989:107). Finally, the 19 nature reserves that had existed at the beginning of the Cultural Revolution in 1965 increased to more than 1,000 by the year 2000, along with 187 natural parks (Weller 2006:77).

Taken together, this statistical data on the rapid development of tourism and heritage industries illustrates the extent to which cultural and environmental preservation have become aspects of state policy during the reform period. This is not to dismiss the pressing preservationist and environmental concerns evident in China. Yet what is arguably the most rapid state-directed modernization campaign in history has included a dramatic transformation of cultural industries, significant investments in preservation, and the state invention of a neologism (*yichan*) to promote a concept (heritage) that had not previously existed. What is behind this national campaign to promote and preserve the past, a campaign guided by a political party that in previous generations actively supported the *destruction* of this same past?

Cultural Heritage and State Building

As already noted, heritage programs, policies, and campaigns are inherently political, focusing as they do on shaping particular narratives about the past for contemporary purposes. Rather than being the outcome of a neutral process of collecting important cultural objects and/or sites, heritage is produced for specific reasons through deliberate actions and particular choices (Ashworth 1994:27). This political base is nevertheless easily obscured by foregrounding technical questions of physical preservation and aesthetic questions of protecting cultural objects and practices from economic forces.

Though international organizations such as UNESCO have lauded the Chinese state promotion of cultural preservation and nature conservation, politics plays a crucial role in this process. Just as an official discourse of multiculturalism serves to depoliticize political claims of cultural differences (Gladney 2004), heritage projects aim to encapsulate all aspects of a generalized past as elements of an apolitical and generic Chinese heritage (Hevia 2001:222). The Maoist intent during the Cultural Revolution to erase the past has been replaced by a focus on shaping material culture into a leisure commodity, one which, however, clearly carries political intentions. In other words, the erasure not of the past but of historically specific contexts of particular aspects of the past guides the heritage industries in China.

Chinese state heritage policies aim to harness a contested past as a source of allegorical allusions to the present. This allows contemporary authorities to project national roots into an imagined unified past, thereby justifying contemporary national boundaries (Errington 1998:37). State support for the preservation of cultural heritage is therefore useful from a governance perspective because it strengthens state legitimacy, both domestically and internationally (Tuohy 1991:201).

Having abandoned communism as an immediate policy goal, the Communist Party rules through a depoliticized process framed around development (*fazhan*) and modernization (*xiandai zhuyi*). The Party positions itself as both provider of the benefits and promises of modernization (what CCP officials refer to as the *material* base of development) and as protector of citizens from modernization's supposed evils, cultural degradation and the perceived chaos of economic change (the *spiritual* base of development).

Figure 2.1 Qing Summer Resort, Chengde, Hebei Province.

The enthusiastic acceptance of the UNESCO project of world heritage by Chinese state authorities fits a state and party projection of what Tim Oakes terms a "landscape of nostalgia" (1997:42). As noted above, the 1982 Heritage Conservation Act specifically called for the preservation of the built heritage of the People's Republic to promote and strengthen nationalism, modernization, and socialism (Sofield and Li 1998:370–371). This nationalist vision, which downplays and often ignores a previous state emphasis on historical sites related to the Communist Party and Civil War, now actively promotes the "four olds" (culture, customs, habits, and ideas), the target of Red Guards and radicalized youth during the Cultural Revolution. This shift in focus seeks to link contemporary society to an imagined past of seamless Han unity as well as to non-Han cultural regions of the current PRC as an historic "China" (Denton 2005:570). In the process, "China" is produced as a unified territory of like-minded citizens spanning thousands of years of history. This claim of an unbroken four thousand year historical record is not just found in state rhetoric but also in Chinese academic writing on heritage issues (cf. Liu 1983; Zhuang 1989).

For example, the official application for World Heritage status for the Potala Palace in Lhasa states that this site deserves inclusion not because it symbolizes Tibet nationhood or Tibetan culture but because it "embodies the outstanding skills of the Tibetan, Han, Mongol, Man, and other nationalities and the high achievements of Tibetan architecture in terms of the overall layout of the Palace as well as its civil engineering, its metalwork, its sculptures, and its wall paintings" (UNESCO 1993:1). In other words, the Potala was deemed significant because it reflects the joint technical and aesthetic achievements of the *peoples* of China, not of a separate nation of Tibet. This foregrounding of national unity is what one also finds in the official application for World Heritage status put forward for the Qing Dynasty imperial grounds at Chengde, northwest of Beijing, despite the historical fact that the Manchurian royal family explicitly designed this resort area as a retreat from Beijing and their Chinese subjects, not as a symbol of Chinese culture (Hevia 2001:224).

Following the extension of heritage status to Lhasa's Jokhang Temple in 2000 and Norbulinka Summer Palace in 2001, UNESCO authorities expressed their official concern with intensive redevelopment in the Barkhor historic area, which includes the Potala Palace and Jokhang Temple. UNESCO was particularly concerned with the construction of a thirteen-story public security complex in the area and the renovation of the Shol neighborhood in front of the Potala. Their response, however, was limited to a request for further meetings with Chinese state authorities (UNESCO 2002:30) and praise for the transformation of Shol into an "Exhibition Complex of Tibetan Folk Arts" (UNESCO 2005:4).

This UNESCO response to how state authorities manage the built space of the Barkhor area is understandable in the context of Tibet's political reality. For some officials, pragmatically accepting preservation of tangible cultural sites on any terms undoubtedly is better than no preservation. This perspective is especially relevant in the case of Tibet, given that Chinese authorities oversaw the destruction of many Tibetan cultural sites during the initial occupation of Tibet in the 1950s and 1960s and during the Cultural Revolution of 1966–1976. UNESCO's response avoids politics altogether, instead focusing on the need for better signage highlighting the "World Heritage Values of the Potala Palace" and suggesting ways to "address the challenge of tourism pressure" by diverting tourists to a proposed visitor center (UNESCO 2005:4).

The case of Lhasa's historic sites points to a practical dilemma for UNESCO and other groups seeking to support the preservation of tangible material culture sites and intangible cultural and social practices. To do so, they must sometimes work with state authorities who have little interest in maintaining authentic cultural differences and identities or in preserving sites in the name of universal culture and peace. The paradox that shapes the relationship between UNESCO and Chinese state authorities is unavoidable: UNESCO marks sites as worthy of protection because of their universal cultural and historical value, while Chinese authorities situate these sites as elements in the state narrative of Chinese culture and civilization.

ORDERING HUMAN SUBJECTS

The Chinese government classifies the peoples of China into five "races" (*zu*), Han, Manchurian, Mongolian, Tibetan, and Muslim, and fifty-one minority peoples (*shao shu minzu*). Each official minority group is classified by territory, language, means of production, and customs, and the nation is deemed the source of culture and civilization. According to this logic, peoples such as Tibetans and Mongolians are recognized as different from Han Chinese not simply because they have a different language and script but also because they have "traditions." These traditions in turn impede them from becoming modern (Blum 2000:98).

This positioning of minority peoples as less developed and following in the footsteps of a more advanced "race" is rooted in the stage-based social evolutionary model of late nineteenth century anthropologist Lewis Henry Morgan and the early-twentieth-century historical materialism of Joseph Stalin. Morgan's three stages of social development (savagery, barbarism, and civilization) were transformed in the Soviet Union into a five-stage theory of development that all societies pass through: primitive communism, slavery, feudalism, capitalism, and socialism.

This Soviet model of social evolution and development in turn became in post-1949 China the theoretical basis for classifying minority peoples (Yang 1996:96–97).

However, this political focus on managing diversity at a folk-cultural level while promoting national unity also reflects popular assumptions among Han Chinese about the relationship of Han with others, particularly a widely held belief that diverse folkways are subsumed within a broader, shared civilization with the Han people at its center (Tuohy 1991:214). The concept of being "Han" in the sense of nationality or ethnicity (*minzu*) or the notion of being "Chinese" (*zhongguo ren*) are relatively recent identity markers, dating from the decades leading up to the 1911 Nationalist Revolution (Gladney 2004:14). *Minzu*, for example, first appeared in print only in 1874 (Zhang 1997). The first of Sun Yatsen's "Three Principles of the People" (*Sanmin Zhuyi*), it is a neologism coined from the Japanese *minzokushugi* and connotes a sense of racial difference and hence racial nationalism (Tuttle 2005:58; see also Dikőtter 1992).

Before the 1911 Revolution, time was marked regnally, taking the ascension year of a ruler as a starting point. For example, the first Opium War (1839–1842) between the United Kingdom and the Qing Empire began from the Qing perspective not in 1839 but in the nineteenth year of the Emperor Daoguang's reign. Inhabitants of the Empire were subjects of the Emperor, not citizens of a country called China; for common people, "the empire was not a country but the country, not a culture but culture itself" (Harrison 2000:7). Personal identity was rooted in one's family, clan, or village, while social relations at the most abstract level separated not citizens or subjects of different states, kingdoms, or empires, but people who were civilized and barbarians (*yi*). In this Sinocentric worldview, to be civilized meant to have access to written language (Chinese), which in turn provided people with the ability to learn and understand how to be human by studying the foundational texts of Confucianism (Zhang 1997:75). Barbarians, on the other hand, were regarded as less than fully human, reflected in the animal radicals used to classify them linguistically (Dikötter 1992:8). The implication is that someone who was Chinese was someone who was civilized. "Chinese" was thus not a biological category possessed by dint of birth but a cultural category that was attained through education and enculturation.

The cultural basis of Chineseness is precisely what Sun Yatsen sought to transform in his critique of the Qing Dynasty and call for a revolution. Sun believed a revolution could succeed only if the subjects of the Empire possessed a sense of both racial identity and nationalism. He argued that the majority of Qing subjects had to first be convinced that their identity was tied to the ethnic marker "Han" and not to local place or language differences. Only then would they recognize that the Manchu-centered Qing Dynasty was a foreign occupier and hence no different than the Europeans who were seeking to carve out territories within China (Wei et al. 1994:42–43). And only then would Qing subjects recognize themselves as citizens (*guomin*, "people of a nation") of a republic and not subjects of an empire (Harrison 2000:175). Once the Revolution had succeeded, however, Dr. Sun called on Han people to become "Chinese" by joining with non-Han groups to form a new nation:

> Now, in overthrowing the Manchus and restoring the Han nation, we have achieved only the negative half of the goal of nationalism. From now on, we must struggle to boldly advance toward the positive side of that goal. What is this positive goal? It is for the Han people to sacrifice the separate nationality, history, and identity they are so proud of and to merge with all sincerity with the Manchus, Mongols, Muslims, and Tibetans in one melting pot to create a new order of Chinese nationalism. (Sun 1912, quoted in Wei et al. 1994:225)

Just as Han were to lead non-Han groups down a pathway of national progress and development in a Republican China that would unite ethnic groups, Han under Chairman Mao were constituted as the vanguard of the Socialist Revolution, charged with assisting non-Han groups to march forward into a Marxist future (Gladney 2004:13). Consequently, between 1949 and 1957, the central government funded ethnographic surveys and field work in minority areas; established minority research institutes in Beijing, Kunming, Lanzhou, Guiyang, Chengdu, Ürümqi, and Hohhot; oversaw the creation of writing systems for minority groups; and classified minority cultural practices and modes of production. The overall goal was to document minority practices before these disappeared as China was transformed into a socialist state (Zhang 1997).

The state-directed projects of becoming modern that Sun Yatsen and the Chinese Nationalist Party (KMT) undertook after 1911 and that Chairman Mao and the Chinese Communist Party (CCP) undertook after 1949 share cultural assumptions of what it means to be modern. Regarding official minority groups, their relative modernity was tied to their cultural distance, real or perceived, from Han (Oakes 1997:46), in particular the Uyghur peoples of western China and Tibetans (Gladney 2004; Blum 2000). At the same time, all the peoples of China were imagined to belong to a single family, enriching each other:

> Chinese history and culture are remarkable for the unity between these groups. In this big community, the cultures of the various nationalities interact and help to promote each other; at the same time they continually

> enrich their own heritage with elements from the culture of other countries. (Liu 1983:15)

This process of being and becoming modern continues in postsocialist China. After the chaos of the Cultural Revolution years when the Party encouraged the wholesale destruction of cultural differences, "culture" has been transformed into a development resource. For example, an emphasis on tourism as a development tool in minority areas intersects with how non-Han residents of these areas are both officially and popularly imagined in the state's ongoing drive to modernization. Because minority peoples are assumed to be less modern than Han Chinese, they are (or should be) grateful for Han help in becoming modern, given that modernization is unavoidable to become advanced (Blum 2000:73–74). In like manner, tangible cultural sites in both minority and Han locales are now viewed by local officials as development resources. In other words, from the local state perspective, religious temples and other cultural sites at places such as Wutai Shan should be protected and promoted not because they are heritage sites important to the world at large, but because they are heritage *resources*. Hence protection and preservation are of less concern than accessibility and wealth generation. The Maoist utopian goal of erasing cultural differences and constructing world socialist citizens has been jettisoned by the Party, replaced by a policy aimed at managing these differences (Figure 2.2). Culture and heritage, particularly for minority groups, is now managed as a resource devoid of political content (Hevia 2001:236–237).

This is done in part by arguing against any link between ethnicity and nationalism. For example, in a recent introduction to ethnicity in China, the author asserts that Chinese mistakenly accepted the European concept of nationality in the late nineteenth century (Zhang 2010:8). Citing the work of the American scholar John King Fairbank, Zhang Qian argues that China has never had nationalities but instead has existed for more than three thousand years as a "united multi-ethnic country" tied together by a shared cultural foundation (18). Given this historical fact, ethnic minorities have a right to practice specific customs and traditions (the intangibles of heritage) within the Chinese nation (*zhonghua minzu*). Consequently, displaying and using heritage as a resource will not lend credence to nationalist claims.

The commodification of culture in the service of economic development and national unity is not, however, the only explanation for the explosion of tourism and heritage in China. National identity, political control, and economic development are key elements in this radical transformation of leisure and the past. Nor is heritage the domain only of ethnic minorities; far more Chinese citizens tour Han Chinese areas

Figure 2.2 Tibetan cultural performance, Putuocheng Temple, Chengde, Hebei Province.

and heritage sites than minority areas. And increasing numbers visit rural areas populated not with minorities but by Han Chinese peasants who themselves seek to move, not as tourists but as migrant laborers.

This mass movement of rural migrant laborers to the new centers of modernity and of privileged urban consumers to the rustic centers of "old" China has been made possible by a strategic retreat by the Party-State in its control of citizen mobility. Before economic reforms began in 1979, all citizens were tied economically and socially to either agricultural collectives or state enterprises, and any sort of travel required official permission. This control was possible because all transportation and hotel services were state controlled and access required official documentation. However, economic reform policies spurred a demand for low-cost manual laborers in production zones along the east coast. At the same time, the elimination of agricultural collectives and creation of a lease-holding land system created a large surplus labor pool in the countryside. The net result was the emergence for the first time in Chinese history of a significant migrant labor class that today numbers approximately 150 million (Lee 2007).

China today is a country in which two groups have become mobile: a marginalized peasant class of factory hands, construction workers, nannies, street vendors, and other occupations that increasingly affluent urban residents no longer want to do, and a small but influential urban consumer class with the disposable income and leisure time to tour. These two classes of mobile subjects are connected not just by economic reforms but also by the Party's focus on cultivating a modern sensibility, what in Chinese is referred to as a "civilized" (*wenming*) consciousness as demonstrated by personal "quality" (*suzhi*). Thus, just as rural migrant workers are lauded for contributing to national economic development goals, they are also tasked with bringing an increased level of civilization back to their rural communities. In like manner, domestic tourism is supposed to raise the levels of civility of both tourists and local residents of toured sites (Nyíri 2009:154). Just as the middle class is supposed to serve as a model for proper modern behavior in urban areas, whether in the public or private spheres, the act of touring is aimed at a similar purpose. Urban tourists will increase their own *suzhi* (in this context, cultural capital) by visiting heritage sites, while at the same time modeling proper *suzhi* (in the sense of civility and civilized behavior) for local residents.

State-encouraged tourism at heritage sites thus has several objectives. At the local level (the primary source of funding for heritage projects), economic growth, job creation, and control of new forms of wealth creation are goals; at the national level, shaping historical narratives to serve contemporary political objectives is a target. But just as important from the national perspective is the promotion of a new class of citizen-subjects disciplined to be modern in an appropriate manner.

In the remainder of this chapter, I analyze the connections between tourism promotion, heritage preservation, and national moral campaigns to shape behavior, cultivate a civilized consciousness, and develop a modern sensibility. While the Communist Party now emphasizes individual success as measured by wealth accumulation through engagement with market forces rather than egalitarianism and collective development, the underlying policy goal remains the same: modernization. This objective preceded the People's Republic and can be traced back to the 1911 Revolution. As with late Qing reformers and Sun Yatsen himself, the Party emphasizes modernization not just in a tangible, material sense but also in an intangible spiritual (*jingshen*) sense. That is to say, a material transformation of society is assumed to also require a psychological transformation. Modernity from this perspective is not measured only by statistics such as GDP, trade, and per capita income but also by the presence of a modern consciousness and civilized demeanor. In this sense, the Communist Party is no longer the vanguard of the working class and peasants, but the moral guide of society. This claim to stewardship is shaped by four key terms: quality (*suzhi*), culture (*wenhua*), hygiene (*weisheng*), and civilization (*wenming*).

To provide context to my analysis, I begin with a brief review of the moral project of the Chinese Communist Party since it came to power in

1949. My purpose is to demonstrate a foundational ethical perspective on what it means to be modern that transcends political differences between the *Guomindang* (Chinese Nationalist Party, KMT) and the *Gongchangdang* (Chinese Communist Party, CCP). The CCP's oft-stated emphasis on both the material (*wuzhi*) and spiritual (*jingshen*) basis of modernization links the market-focused leaders of contemporary China with not just the socialist revolutionaries of Chairman Mao's era but also KMT leader Chiang Kaishek's New Life Movement of 1934–1938. All have sought to achieve the aims of Sun Yatsen's Revolutionary League: the modernization of China with, to borrow from the language of the Communist Party, "Chinese characteristics," based on maintaining the essence (*ti*, the root) of what it means to be Chinese.

The Moral Pedagogy of a Revolution

Mao Zedong believed that a society's collective effort could transcend the historical stages of development, linked to specific stages of production, that Karl Marx had argued were both universal and linear. Contrary to orthodox Marxist theory, Mao insisted that China could move from a feudal subsistence agricultural stage of development to a socialist industrial stage by harnessing its collective willpower. To do so, he advocated for a wholesale reordering of society, focused not just on the means of production but also on the spatial organization of everyday life. This spatial transformation in turn was aimed at the moral reordering of Chinese citizens into members of a "national socialist culture" that transcended the Confucian social bonds of family and friends (Anagnost 1994:228). To achieve this goal the Party eliminated private property, nationalized the means of production, and organized urban residents into work units (*danwei*) and peasants into communes.

Work units operated as distinct social and economic spheres, providing members with food, clothing, housing, education, and employment. Citizens were born into, married into, and died in work units. In addition to their role as the state-in-practice, *danwei* served as the primary social web for members and as a foundational aspect of identity (Leung 2000:618). The primary objective of work units was to replace the foundational role family ties had played in Chinese society for thousands of years with a new form of community, a fully rationalized, organized, and planned micro society that simultaneously displaced preferential kin ties and turned social relationships into an aspect of economic production (Bray 2005:96). In doing so, public (*gong*) and private (*si*) distinctions were transformed, the state and public were collapsed into a single category, and the private sphere (literally secret or illicit, historically located within the family) was administratively superseded. The result was the replacement of public-private distinctions, in the form of family and other, with a revolutionary form of public life that contrasted with an abstract general public, the public and state space of the nation (Womack 1991:324).

It would, however, be a mistake to reduce work units to either the most visible form of an all-powerful state or the site of potential resistance to central authority. Instead, they were both produced by state power and the enabler of this power (Bray 2005:96), a type of bureaucratic entity that in its ideal form offered administrative simplification in the form of "insularity without autonomy" (Naughton 1997:181). For the majority of urban residents, personal identity in the not-to-recent past was closely tied to their work units. Work units thus served as a distinct form of society, an experiential space of social reality distinct from both society and the state (Lu and Perry 1997:12). In other words, Lockean distinctions between either state and society or the self and the state make little sense in this context. Instead, individual identity was shaped and constrained by work unit identity, which in turn both shaped and constrained notions of society.

Discussions of the totalitarian power of the Chinese state under Mao tend to assume a state-citizen template of social order, thus ignoring the actual complexities of a *danwei*-rooted society. This view takes as a given both the Lockean notion of autonomous individual citizens and what follows from this, the assumption that a social order based on collective institutions will automatically *not* be attractive to individuals because it binds them socially to employers. It follows from this that workers in a market economy are freer because employers can only fire them from their jobs—not penalize their access to housing, education, food, and other necessities (Womack 1991:321–322). However, these assumptions only hold true if work unit administrators actually were able to use this power. In practice, this was difficult because to do so required finding an alternative work unit assignment for disaffected employees. In this sense, removing an employee was equivalent to an officer trying to "fire" a soldier from an army. In practice, *danwei* administrators and party cadres just as often sought to lessen the impact of Party directives on their members as they served as the eyes of the state. What from a distance appears to have been extreme dependence on work unit authorities and a subsequent lack of personal autonomy was, in the context of socialist China, beneficial and thus desired by many workers, precisely because administrators could not arbitrarily and summarily dismiss employees and, where possible, deflected the most onerous of state demands (Womack 1991:322). The majority of work unit members appear to have accepted what by the 1980s had become a new type of social contract, in which citizens ceded their autonomy to the Party in exchange for lifetime employment, health care, housing, and the promise of social stability (Lee 2007).

Economic reforms that began after the death of Mao in 1976 have brought great changes to work units. Initial reforms that were designed to introduce competition into the production process, increase efficiency, and eliminate nonproductive and inefficient work units had the paradoxical effect of strengthening some forms of work units. Because these initial reforms allowed administrators to keep a larger percentage of the revenue they generated, well-run work units were able to invest in social services and housing for their members, increasing worker dependency (Naughton 1997:183). Indeed, while many industrial enterprises have struggled to adapt to market-driven administrative logic, others, usually service or educational institutions in desirable locales, have thrived.

In retrospect, urban work units and rural communes were as much pedagogical tools as they were political institutions, designed not just to control citizens but also to shape them by instilling a new moral code. Paradoxically, though they were aimed at undermining kin ties (the social glue of Confucianism), these social structures used the foundational premise of Confucianism (that all people can be improved through a combination of social modeling and self-cultivation) as their key organizing principle. This was combined with Mao's belief that the collective willpower of society could enable China to literally leap through material stages of development and thereby achieve authentic communism without passing through a capitalist stage. This utopian belief took concrete form during the Great Leap Forward campaign (1957–1961) and the Great Proletarian Cultural Revolution (1966–1976). During the Great Leap Forward, agricultural land was collectivized, villages transformed into communes, and suspected counterrevolutionaries attacked. The total death toll from famine and political terror was as high as 30 million (Dikötter 2010). After pragmatists scaled back Mao's ideological campaign, he began the Cultural Revolution in 1966, his attempt to eradicate feudal elements in Chinese culture and alleged capitalist sympathizers in the communist party. The resulting violence, destruction, and displacement led to the direct deaths of somewhere between one million and ten million Chinese citizens. As catastrophic as these political campaigns were, it is important to note that each in turn targeted the material (*wuzhi*) and spiritual (*jingshen*) aspects of modernization; just as the Great Leap Forward was supposed to propel the People's Republic to a higher stage of socialist economic development, the Cultural Revolution would emancipate citizens from the shackles of feudal traditions and produce proper socialist beings.

Neither, of course, happened. Instead, Deng Xiaoping gained power after Mao's death in 1976 and shifted state policies away from constant revolution and ideological purity to economic pragmatism and managed growth. The rejection of Maoism by the CCP has provided citizens with limited personal autonomy and a measure of control over their own lives. Indeed, the extent to which Chinese citizens can exercise some form of personal agency relative to the social reality of China before 1989 is often overlooked by foreign critics of the CCP. Moreover, though everyday life may have not been completely depoliticized in China, it certainly has been de-ideologicized. After the campaigns that caused such chaos, destruction, death, and personal trauma between 1957 and 1989, a life of mass consumption and apolitical apathy has been arguably quite appealing to many, at least in the short term. But this has left a vacuum. If the Communist Party no longer is an advocate of communism, or even socialism, on what basis does it continue to justify its rule? Does the implicit social contract between the Party and citizens that replaced the former Maoist social contract simply provide people with the right to own private property, to travel and choose jobs, and to have personal privacy in exchange for public acceptance of Party rule? If making money, traveling, and shopping are the only "rights" citizens have, how long can the Party maintain control? And what does this indicate about the moral and ethical basis of the existing political system?

Spiritual Civilization

The CCP has responded to this legitimacy dilemma by jettisoning Mao's radical (and profoundly non-Marxist) interpretation of the relationship between a society's base and superstructure (Anagnost 1997:84). Mao had rejected the fundamental Marxist point that a society's material base (its stage of development) determined its social development (its superstructure), instead arguing that the collective will of the Chinese could transform the base itself, thus fast-tracking China's advance toward communism. Deng began the reform process by shifting the political focus away from class struggle towards general prosperity (*xiaokang shehui*), based on a stable material and spiritual civilization (*wenming*). That is to say, although he radically transformed the economic basis of Chinese society by embracing (limited) private market action, he did not intend to allow market forces to shape social and moral behavior. Deng thus was as much a heretical Marxist as was Mao. While Mao had attempted to use the superstructure to transform the base, Deng sought to prevent the base from transforming the superstructure.

Deng's reforms thus mirror to some extent the aims of, ironically, the reformist elements in the late Qing Dynasty, who sought to *zhonghua xiyong*, to use Western technology, ideas, and products while maintaining the cultural essence of "Chineseness" (Dynon 2008:86). Deng also promoted the first Spiritual Civilization Campaign (*jingshen wenhua yundong*) in 1982. This was not the first moral campaign the CCP launched. Between 1949 and 1957, the Party had promoted model student, family, and work unit campaigns along with various hygiene campaigns that focused on pests, garbage, and public behavior such as spitting (Li 1987:38–39). The 1982 campaign, however, was quite unlike those of the Maoist era. Absent were the ideological and class elements that had encouraged and caused so much suffering and death. An emphasis on social behavior replaced a discourse of revolutionary purity and the supremacy of the working class. Instead of demanding a collective great leap forward or acceptance of the cult of Mao, the Party promoted public morality (*gongde*), patriotism (*aiguo zhuyi*), culture (*wenhua*), discipline (*jilu*), and ideals (*lixiang*). Serving as a new base for all of these points was the term "civilization" itself.

The second Spiritual Civilization Campaign was begun in 1996 by Jiang Zemin, the former party leader of Shanghai who rose to power in the wake of the Tiananmen Square violence in the spring of 1989. Whereas Deng's 1982 campaign had at least made a pro forma recognition of the role of collectivization in Chinese society, Jiang's 1996 campaign replaced the language of socialism with that of cultural nationalism (Dynon 2008:93). This was followed in 2004 by President Hu Jintao's call for a harmonious society based not just on material, spiritual, and political advancement but also "ecological civilization" (106–107).

In 1997, the State Council established the Central Commission for Building Spiritual Civilization (*zhongyang jingshen weming jianshe zhidao weiyuanwei*). It was given three responsibilities: improving technical aspects of life, increasing public awareness of the law, and promoting physical fitness and hygiene. More broadly, however, this commission was tasked with overseeing the cultural engineering (*wenhua gongcheng*) of society (Tomba 2009:606). To do so, it promotes idealized middle-class social norms as models of behavior for peasants and workers under the rubric of civilization.

Unlike in countries such as the United States, the term "civilized" has not disappeared from public use in China as society has advanced materially. Quite the opposite: exhortations to be civilized, act civilized, and live as a member of a civilized household are found throughout society, on banners, billboards, and television, in parks, restrooms, rail stations, and other public venues. Michel Foucault's dictum that the disciplining of the self becomes increasingly invisible in modernizing societies has little relevance to the realities of contemporary China, where prescriptive rules describing how to be civilized are both highly visible and visibly ritualized (Anagnost 1994).

This civilization campaign has both an Enlightenment and Confucianist base, which reflects the more than one-hundred-year debate among

Chinese intellectuals across the political spectrum about how to be simultaneously modern and Chinese. *Wenming* is not actually a Chinese word but a cultural borrowing from Meiji Japan (Friedman 2004) and entered the Chinese language at approximately the same time period as the equally ambiguous terms *minzu*, variously translated as "ethnicity," "race," and "clan," *fengjian mixin*, "feudal superstition," and *wenhua* "culture" (Erbaugh 2008:639). Like its Japanese equivalent *bunmei*, *wenming* has two distinct connotations, one mental and spiritual and the other material (Anagnost 1997:82), which in turn reflects a split between Eastern (*dongfang*) and Western (*xifang*) orientations (Lee 1999:44). For the former, *wenming* refers to what is often described by state officials as well as Han Chinese citizens as a unified history of thousands of years, making China unique in the world. As noted above, this claim of a homogeneous history has taken on the aura of a discursive truth, a commonsense view that ignores centuries of interactions between different linguistic groups within what today constitutes the People's Republic. Chinese member delegates of ICOMOS, for example, begin their report on cultural heritage conservation in China by stating, "China is a unified country of many ethnic groups; it is a vast country with a vast history and an unbroken cultural tradition" (Agnew and Demas 2004:59).

But this term also describes an always-becoming *civil* society that signals not an unbroken historical narrative but an emerging present and future rooted in the flux of modernity. This is a starkly different view of society from the one European and American proponents of civil society and good governance imagined. For the latter, civil society is the oft-stated goal of development programs aimed at promoting democracy, human rights, and the rule of law. Proponents of this perspective believe that a civil society (a society filled with nonstate organizations) is crucial to check the power of the state, cultivate ethnic and social tolerance, and eventually encourage the development of material security for its members. The Chinese term *wenming*, however, signifies a society of productive, socially responsible, and increasingly self-disciplined citizens who understand how to check their individual behavior to assist state leaders with the development of a materially and spiritually modern society (Friedman 2004:691). *Wenming* communicates both a historical basis of development and a contemporary sense of what it means to be modern and Chinese. "To be civilized" in this sense is to be productive and efficient, but far more: it is to practice proper hygiene, manners, family habits, and thinking (Nyiri 2006b:88).

The moral attributes of *suzhi* (quality) and *wenhua* (culture) guide this ideal civil society. The analytical interpretations of *suzhi* vary widely. It has been dismissed as code language for the extraction of labor from peasants under the guide of modernization (Yan 2003), located at the nexus of nutritional, educational, and child-rearing discourses (Anagnost 2004), and critiqued as a Foucaldian attempt to discipline a new class of neoliberal subjects (Kipnis 2007:385). Yet until the late 1970s, *suzhi* conveyed a sense of inborn character, in contrast to *suyang*, one's embodied or learned character. Used in this sense, a person's bad character might be blamed on either family background or lack of education. However, with the imposition of a national one-child policy in 1978, state authorities redefined and assiduously promoted *suzhi* as not an inborn attribute but as a broader qualitative measurement of social worth as embodied by a person's relative development (Kipnis 2006:299–300). Those who possess a high level of *suzhi* thus possess proper (physical) health, (mental) intelligence, and (moral) character, attributes that have Marxist and Confucianist foundations as well as holistic practices such as various martial arts and exercise forms (Jacka 2009). Qigong, gongfu, wushu, and most recently falun gong are not aimed at either physical or mental well-being but seek to simultaneously cultivate one's moral, mental, and physical well-being.

To possess *suzhi* is to be simultaneously modern and Chinese, while to possess *wenhua* is to possess (Chinese) culture and not be simply Westernized. *Suzhi* is thus a measure of one's cultural level and hence degree of modernity. It is evoked in an array of social issues, ranging from family planning, nutrition, medicine, and physical fitness to personal hygiene, self-improvement, education policies, local governance, and, increasingly, consumer choices in housing, clothing, and lifestyles. Those who possess proper quality and culture are capable of self-governance (*zizhi*), while those with low quality are targeted for improvement (Tomba 2009:595). This is reflected in a very public and relentless State and Party emphasis on quality education (*suzhi jiaoyu*) and the production of high-quality citizens (Kipnis 2006:300).

"Quality" and "culture" are not just key words of the Party but just as important of an emerging middle class because progress and social awareness are no longer seen as emanating from the experiences of the peasantry and working class, as during the Maoist era, but from those citizens who possess higher quality. This repositioning of the middle and upper classes as role models for advancement is a sharp break from the class politics of Mao's era, when anyone with kin ties to intellectuals, capitalists, or the petty bourgeoisie experienced ostracism or worse. Mao's idealization of the peasantry and anti-intellectualism reached its height shortly after the Cultural Revolution began when he promoted the resettlement of urban youth in rural areas to learn from peasants.[2] Far from being subjects to be reshaped into revolutionaries, middle-class Chinese are now lauded by Party theorists as role models for a modern

China. Being civil and civilized is now a matter of education and social standing, not of class background or revolutionary credentials (Anagnost 1997:86). Therefore, the vanguard of a future society of material wealth, social stability, and proper moral character is no longer the working class and peasantry but the emerging bourgeoisie.

Modernization theory suggests that it is just a matter of time before newly empowered consumers demand to also become politically empowered citizens. The Market, according to this perspective, will create its own revolutionary class of consumer-actors who will in turn transform China into a liberal democratic society. This assumption remains a key aspect of American trade policies with the People's Republic. It is so powerful and largely unquestioned that as a political principle it has remained unchallenged since the Carter Administration. Liberal and neoliberal Democrats, conservative and neoconservative Republicans have shared it. Increasingly, however, researchers point to the fact that Chinese society shows little if any evidence of such a middle-class political consciousness (cf. Dixon 2003).

Far from being either the enemy of the people or the Communist Party, the emerging middle- and upper-class elites are of crucial importance in the construction of what the Party defines as a *Chinese* modern society. This new elite does not necessarily contest either the State or the Party because it is part of both the State and Party moral project of development (Jacka 2009:526). Indeed, the State promotes the newly affluent as the vanguard of a modern and harmonious (*hexie*) society, one in which self-governance within a Party-state has replaced the Maoist totalitarian state (Tomba 2009:593–595). Far from contesting the current governmental focus on cultivating civilization and lifting the quality of the masses, many emerging elites share this goal (Nyiri 2006b:88).

This Party shift from a transformation of the social body to the reshaping of individuals does not signal a turn toward liberal notions of autonomous actors. Instead, this emphasis on cultivating and producing higher quality citizens is a turn back to the early decades of the Chinese Revolution. This civilization campaign is eerily similar to what the Nationalist Party (KMT) advocated in the 1930s when they launched China's first cultural revolution, the New Life Movement (*xin shenghuo yundong*).

Cleansing the Body Politic: The KMT and the Moral Remaking of China

In February 1934, Chiang Kaishek, military and political leader of the Republic of China, announced a campaign aimed at a moral reawakening of society. Emphasizing hygiene and personal behavior, the New Life

Movement was both conservative and revolutionary, designed to replace mass political action with a State and Party-directed mass social movement. The goal was not to empower people but to mobilize broad support for KMT efforts to modernize Chinese society by strengthening its moral base. It thus was designed to counter both the radical class-based social critique of the Chinese Communist Party and the bourgeois criticism of the New Culture Movement (Dirlik 1975). According to the former, China could only be saved by defeating foreign imperialism and eradicating feudal institutions and social relationships, while for the latter, eradicating Confucianism would liberate individuals to embrace scientific knowledge and personal liberty. For both, morality was a central issue (Lu 2007).

According to Chiang Kaishek, Chinese were lazy, decrepit, filthy, and hedonistic; they smoked, drank, and gambled too much, thought of prostitution as simply a commercial transaction, urinated in public, and believed in ghosts (cited in Dirlik 1975:954). An "anything goes" (*suibian*) attitude dominated all social classes, and few people cared for or had any consideration for others (975). To combat these character flaws, he outlined a moral code based on what he called the "four virtues": consciousness, clarity, propriety, and logical reason. These virtues in turn would promote patriotism, morality, a broad social awareness, and self-discipline ("Foreign News" 1934). This moral reawakening campaign rested on the central Confucian principle of self to other: individual striving towards betterment would serve as a model for others to follow, thus moving from the simple (the individual body) to the complex (the social body). Chiang Kaishek asserted that cultivating these four central virtues would promote what he called the "art" of proper, civilized conduct, which in turn would lead to a stable social order (Chiang 1934 in de Bary and Lufrano 2001:342–344). He linked the act of becoming modern for both individuals and society to the cultivation of "Chineseness," what the Chinese Communist Party now refers to as the spiritual basis of development and modernization.

For both the KMT under Chiang Kaishek and the current CCP, the health of society is reflected not only by the health of the individual but also in personal and social hygiene, which in turn is emblematic of both individual and social morality. The Chinese term for hygiene (*weisheng*) connotes much more than personal physical cleanliness or sanitation. A literal translation of the term is "to guard life," yet it is used in the context of both a personal and social sense of health, fertility, and internal balance (Rogaski 2004:15). Like *wenming*, *weisheng* has become a visible marker of modernization in contemporary China as individual households as well as neighborhoods, shops, factories, schools, and even entire cities are recognized as civilized and hygienic.

The roots of *weisheng* are found in Confucius' *Analects* (Chapter 10), where he advocates moderation in choice, and in the Daoist classic *Zhuangzi* (Chapter 23), in which the Daoist sage Laozi describes the secrets of preserving life (23–25). In the latter, Laozi responds to his follower Nanrong Chu's questions about guarding life by suggesting he avoid preferential bonds:

> By conforming to nature, the perfect men share the food with the earth and the joy with the heaven. They do not entangle themselves in intricate human relationships, or blame each other or plot against each other, or work against each other. They leave without worry and come without care. This is the way to preserve your life. (Zhuangzi 1999:393)

An emphasis on health as a process of guarding life, or preventive medicine combined with a preventive lifestyle, was the defining characteristic of *weisheng* for more than two thousand years. But the New Life Movement of the 1930s promoted a very different type of *weisheng*, what Rogaski (2004) terms "hygienic modernity." It took as a model the Dingxian Mass Education Movement near Beijing, established in 1925 by James Yen, a doctor associated with Peking Union Medical College. Yen's association trained village health workers to provide basic first aid, give vaccinations, supervise public drinking wells, and promote pit latrines and other sanitary measures. His goal was the remaking of peasants into *weisheng*-conscious citizens:

> We are trying to develop not just rural education alone, or rural health, or economic improvement, or citizenship . . . but to coordinate and correlate all these various aspects of community improvement and social upbuilding for the remaking of the Chinese *hsien* [county] and the Chinese citizen. (quoted in Yip 1992:404)

China's first Ministry of Health was established in 1928, shortly after Nationalist military forces under the command of Chiang Kaishek had reunified the country. Health officials confronted a largely rural society that had staggering annual mortality rates: 250/1000 for infants, 25–30/1000 overall. The most common causes of death were communicable but preventable diseases such as typhoid, malaria, cholera, dysentery, tuberculosis, small pox, and diphtheria (Yip 1992:396–397).

The New Life Movement was launched at the same time that the KMT began to revive Confucianism, which had been harshly attacked both within the Party and by outsiders after the 1911 Revolution as the primary cause of China's nineteenth-century decline. For example, a February 1927 edict issued by KMT authorities described Confucianism as "superstitious and out of place in the modern world" and called for the destruction of Confucian temples (Li 1987:17). Yet within a few years, textbooks such as the *Primer for a National Citizen of the Republic* (*Gonghe Guomin Duben*), a standard public school text, cited Confucius as well as medical science to instruct students in how to be moral citizens (Lee 1999:53). This return to Confucius was not, however, part of a restorative political movement designed to reconstitute the social structures of prerevolutionary society. It was instead an attempt to restore what the KMT believed to be proper moral behavior (the essence [*ti*] of Chineseness) as a foundation for a modern citizen-subject (Li 1987; Dirlik 1975). That is, the New Life Movement used selective moral prescriptive categories associated with Confucianism to serve as the social base of a modern Chinese society, one which would suppress self-interest for the good of the nation and state:

> Individual moral improvement was the means to simultaneous and total organization of society, while the constant renewal of individuals was the key to the continued effectiveness of political institutions in an environment in constant flux. (Dirlik 1975:968)

This selective Confucianism ultimately required complete obedience to the State and Party, which logically contradicted Confucius's emphasis on not serving unethical leaders. The KMT sought to construct productive citizens who would be efficient, organized, and ethical, yet would not question the legitimacy of the system. To do so, the New Life Movement prescribed what and how people should eat; what they should wear; how they should sit, stand, walk, dress, greet each other—even clean their noses. Its main impact, however, was on the small minority of citizens who already identified with modernity, particularly urban elites. Widespread famine, food security concerns, and the side effects of civil conflict made good manners and morals irrelevant to many (Li 1987:36; see also Rogaski 2004). By the end of 1935, the New Life Movement was active in nineteen provinces and more than one thousand counties, but by 1937 was effectively over.

The failure of the New Life Movement has been dismissed as a propaganda campaign launched at a time when the KMT was simultaneously trying to eliminate its communist opponents and prevent a complete occupation of China by Japanese military forces. Yet failure does not necessarily mean that party leaders were not sincere in their desires to reshape the moral and social base of Chinese society (Dirlik 1975:953). This campaign was not just a clumsy attempt by a weak government to impose social control. It was instead aimed at achieving precisely what the current Spiritual Civilization Campaigns have sought: a wholesale modernization of society within an ethical and cultural framework of Chinese civilization. Much like China today, in the 1930s, this goal was shared by an emerging civil society of bureaucrats, professionals, and middle-class consumers, all of whom sought to build a modern China by erasing the perceived gap in modernity between their country and foreigners, specifically Europeans and Americans (Rogaski 2004:250). This is reflected in how the movement was viewed at the time by government officials, who lauded the hygienic order it had supposedly established:

> Public health programs are being carried out. The orderly behavior of the people has aroused much favorable comment. There is no wandering or shuffling about the streets, no stopping in the middle of the road, no gaping about and no blocking the traffic. The people abide by what is described as a one-side-of-the-street traffic; that is, they always keep to the left when walking about the streets. Smoking in the streets is considered undesirable and slovenly. Spitting in public places calls for a reprimand, not from the police but from the followers of the New Life Movement. Rudeness and vulgar manners have been, or are being eliminated. (Chen 1936; cited in Dirlik 1975:950)

This moral campaign was not designed to lead to a democratic society in which social and political order was contested through multiparty elections. Indeed, despite the supposed centrality of democracy in Sun Yatsen's *Three Principles of the People*, it is clear from his writings that what he meant was a guided social order that would have more in common with a corporate democracy such as fascism than with liberal democracy:

> Let the great political force of the state be divided into two: the power of the government and the power of the people. Such a division will make the government the machinery and the people the engineer. (Sun 1924, quoted in de Bary and Lufrano 2001:324)

Development as Civilizing Mission

Dr. Sun, glorified by KMT leaders after his death as the "father of the country" (*guofu*), was also the spiritual voice of a state-directed development project that continues to this day (Kirby 2000:139). Sun's advocacy of a Republic based on racial nationalism, centralized authority, and economic and social security; Chiang Kaishek's New Life Movement; and the spiritual civilization campaigns the Chinese Communist Party undertook beginning in 1982 share a Confucian belief in the efficacy of social order, moral education, and an assumed link between external action and internal reflection (Li 1987).

This century-long development project has aimed at the holistic transformation of Chinese people into modern subjects, materially and spiritually, as well as physically, mentally, and morally. It is a project that draws on Confucian concepts of self-improvement and social role modeling, Marxist notions of stage-based development, and a wide array of popular cultural practices found throughout Chinese history. In its most current form, spiritual civilization, it has stressed (literally) the "Five Stresses": civility (*wenming*), courtesy (*limao*), public health (*weisheng*), social order (*chengxu*), and morality (*daode*) (Erbaugh 2008:642). The ambiguity of *wenming* is its strength, transforming whatever this concept is attached to, be this a public restroom, household or work unit, corporation, or heritage site, into an "ideological and moral imperative" (Dynon 2008:107). *Wenming* thus functions in a remarkably similar way to the ambiguous English term, "development." Both *wenming* and development are deployed as seemingly apolitical, nonideological concepts that are often underscrutinized because of their implicit moral authority. In addition, both terms categorize particular subjects as their targets, not a general population, and each is the domain of particular other subjects, those who are considered developed and those who are already civilized. What links these two concepts together is their shared targets, the less developed and the backward.

However, where they differ is in their foundational perspectives on their chosen subjects and hence their implied outcomes. Development practitioners imagine a society of developed individuals who are developed because they function as rational choice-driven autonomous actors. In such a society, a person's original class status will not matter because this can be transcended. In the context of China, a civilized society from the Party perspective might well mean much the same thing, albeit with a moral element that serves to check individual action for the greater good. However, the contemporary neoliberal basis of development is not necessarily shared by middle- and upper-class Chinese citizens. Neoliberalism assumes that social and economic class realities do not matter because these can be transcended through hard work and individual effort. In the context of contemporary China, however, urban residents do not criticize peasants and workers for being lazy but for being low-quality people, a fundamental existential condition that cannot be easily overcome. *Suzhi* discourse and by implication the civilizing process is therefore neither neoliberal nor liberal; it is profoundly illiberal (Kipnis 2007:389–390).

But what is the role of heritage in this ongoing moral and spiritual campaign to shape Chinese citizens into proper modern subjects? In particular, what might be the role of living, experiential heritage, such as that found at a sacred Buddhist site? How does a communist party, officially atheist, promote what the CCP still considers a form of feudal superstition (Buddhist rituals) as an example of not just national heritage but of world heritage? It is to these questions I shall now turn.

Chapter III

"Four Peaks, One River, Five Buddhist Places, and One White Pagoda"

Wutai Shan as a Sacred Site

Two centuries before Buddhism was introduced to China, Wutai Shan was already a sacred site for followers of the Dao, as a place to retreat to from society during the Han Dynasty (206 BCE–220 CE). Approximately seven hundred years later, the rulers of the northern Wei Dynasty (386–534 BCE) began construction of a series of temples dedicated to the Bodhisattva Manjusri (ch. *Wenshu Shuli*) in the valley, and by the late Tang Dynasty (618–907) Wutai Shan, also known as Qingliang Shan, had become a major pilgrimage site for much of East Asia and an important center of Chan Buddhism (Gimello 1992:100). For example, Tibetan King Tri Ralpachen (ruled 817–836) requested woodcut images of Wutai be sent to him in 824, and the famous Japanese monk Ennin (794–864) took paintings of local temples back with him to Japan (Chou 2007:108).

Following the anti-Buddhist campaigns carried out by the late Tang Emperor Wuzong (ruled 840–846), Wutai Shan's influence waned. But In the late-thirteenth century, the Mongolian leader Kublai Khan, founder of the Yuan Dynasty (1271–1368), introduced Tibetan Buddhism to the area, which transformed Wutai into a major pilgrimage destination for Mongolians and Tibetans. This Tibetan presence later expanded greatly under the patronage of the Manchurian Qing Dynasty (1644–1911), which officially endorsed the Gelukpa School of Tibetan Buddhism, using this as a symbol of legitimacy and uniqueness. As with the Qing construction of an Imperial summer resort at Chengde north of Beijing, the Qing patronage of Wutai Shan was aimed at accentuating a claimed ink with Mongolia and the Yuan Dynasty as well as emphasizing Manchu

---

Faith in Heritage: Displacement, Development, and Religious Tourism in Contemporary China by Robert J. Shepherd, 69–89

differences with their Chinese-speaking subjects. In 1659, Tibetan Buddhists were given control of the major religious sites at Wutai, and in 1705, Emperor Kangxi (1654–1722) decreed that ten Mahayana monasteries, including Tayuan, Xiantong, and Pusading, be converted to Tibetan Buddhism (Kohle 2008:78). During the reign of the Qianlong Emperor (1711–1799), these monasteries began to receive direct support from the imperial court (GOC 2008b:117). Wutai Shan also became an imperial destination. For example, between 1683 and 1710, Emperor Kangxi visited the valley five times. However, these were not, strictly speaking, journeys of worship, but more akin to state tours, as the entire court would follow the Emperor to the valley, where he would hunt, banquet, camp, and also visit temples and monasteries. The role of Wutai was thus similar to that of the northeastern city of Jehol (Chengde), site of an extensive summer palace and temple complex built during the reigns of Kangxi and Qianlong. After 1710, occasional imperial visits to Wutai were replaced by annual visits to Jehol. As noted above, both Wutai Shan and Jehol served dual purposes as links between the Manchurian rulers and China's imperial past and as sites that symbolically marked the differences between the Qing and their Chinese subjects. Consequently, the Wutai religious economy flourished during the Qing era. At the time of the 1911 Nationalist Revolution, the valley was home to more than forty major temples and monasteries and several hundred lesser sites, including temples, caves, and shrines sacred to Han Chinese, Mongolians, and Tibetans, scattered about a several hundred kilometer radius.

In the years immediately after the 1911 Revolution, little changed in Wutai. In 1923, an Englishman named Emil Fischer visited the valley with friends in the early winter. They traveled from Beijing to Taiyuan by train, taking advantage of what at that time was the most developed rail line in China. However, at the end of the line, they had to travel for three days by mule to reach Wutai, which Fischer referred to as the "temple city." Mount Wutai, he wrote, "is to the Mongols what Mecca is to the Mohammedans, or Jerusalem is to the Jews" (Fischer 1925:19). Beyond the fact that the temples and monasteries were crowded with Mongolian pilgrims bringing food, silk, and other gifts, Fischer mainly discussed his own discomfort and the weather.

During the war with Japan (1937–1945) and the Chinese civil war (1945–1949), the Wutai valley suffered little damage and saw no major conflicts, although communist guerrillas used the surrounding mountains as sanctuaries. After the 1949 establishment of the People's Republic, the new government placed monasteries and temples under state protection and initially did not forcibly attempt to end religious worship. However, during the collapse of state authority during the Cultural Revolution, monks at the various temples in and around Wutai were beaten, evicted, and in some cases killed, and the temples and monasteries were attacked and damaged by Red Guards. Before this, public worship and pilgrimage had been banned and the surrounding hills stripped of their forests and extensively cultivated in the Great Leap Forward. It was only in the late 1980s that monasteries were allowed to reopen, albeit under strict government control.

The valley currently has 47 functioning monasteries and temples, representing Xianzong (Pure Land) and Mizong (Tibetan) schools. As of 2007, these housed approximately 2,500 Buddhist monks and nuns, according to official data (GOC 2008b:234). However, the unofficial religious population is probably three or four times as high in summer months when Buddhist monks from throughout China converge on Wutai Shan. The area currently has the largest official concentration of religious devotees in China outside Tibet.

Wutai Shan was classified as a national scenic spot (*jingdian*) by the State Council in 1982 and a national forest preserve in 1992. In 1997, it was listed as one of the top thirty-five "elite attractions" in China by the National Tourism Bureau and in 1998 designated a civilized scenic spot (*wenming jingdian*) by the Shanxi Provincial government, which also issued a master plan for development of the area. The entire valley was added to China's tentative list of UNESCO heritage sites in 2001. In this original application, the State Administration of Cultural Heritage (SACH) did not cite Wutai Shan's role as a center of Buddhism as its most important feature. Instead, the nomination was based on its geological importance, unique ecology, value as a meteorological research site, role as a guerrilla base during the anti-Japanese War (1937–1945), and historical contribution to Chinese Buddhism. For the latter, the nomination file emphasized the historical, artistic, and scientific merits of the site, not religious practice (UNESCO 2001). In fact, religious worship was not mentioned at all.

A revised master plan issued in 2005 proposed classifying the entire valley as a national park divided into four zones centered on Taihuai town, site of the most important monasteries and temples. This plan called for the resettlement of Taihuai residents in a new community to be built outside the official park boundaries (GOC 2008a:240–241).[1] Wutai was formally nominated for world heritage status in March 2008, centered on a core zone that included forty Buddhist temples and monasteries, eight of which were classified as "super class": Xiantong, Tayuan, Pusading, Bishan, Shuxiang, Nanshan, Longquan, and Jin'ge (GOC 2008b:35). References to the political importance of Wutai as a revolutionary site for the Communist Party were dropped. However, these were not replaced with a more prominent focus on Buddhism but instead an emphasis on the area's cultural and natural importance. For example, the authors of this report stated that religious buildings demonstrated not the importance of Wutai Shan as a Buddhist pilgrimage site but "Chinese ancient building techniques and art" while Buddhist statues "display Chinese people's genius in art" (14). Moreover, the authors asserted that Wutai was evidence of the "seamless blend of the Chinese and Tibetan cultures" and serves as "an important bridge for cultural exchanges between the Han, Tibetan, Mongolian people and people of other ethnic origins" (UNESCO, 2008b:2). Pilgrimage is referenced, but only in passing and then as a practice of foreign Buddhists and local Tibetans and Mongolians, not Han Chinese (GOC 2008b:27). Instead of Buddhism, the nomination report highlights Wutai Shan's geological and biological characteristics. These include granite-greenstone belts, periglacial landforms, stratigraphical sections, and stromatolite fossils (28–34), as well as its 1,039 vascular bundle plant species, 1,034 angiosperm plants, 160 woody plants, 2,000 insect species, and 142 species of birds (18–20).

Recent history, particularly Chinese Communist Party policies that prohibited religious practice under Mao, is noticeably absent from both this nomination report and the UNESCO evaluation of this application. For example, the authors of the *Nomination Report for Mount Wutai* describe the recent historical context of this site as follows:

> From the late Qing Dynasty to the early years of the Republic of China, Mount Wutai experienced a slow-down due to social instability. Since the founding of the People's Republic of China in 1949 the Central and local governments have been putting into practice the state heritage conservation and religious policies. (GOC 2008b:59)

The UNESCO evaluation report of this application simply repeats this claim, stating that "Mount Wutai declined through social instability" during the last years of the Qing Dynasty and the Republican period (1911–1949), but "since 1949 and the founding of the People's Republic of China, efforts have been directed at reviving and protecting the buildings" (UNESCO 2009:4). This shared perspective ignores the chaos of the Cultural Revolution (1966–1976) and the paradoxes that ensured, such as local workers and peasants defending religious sites at Wutai from marauding urban Red Guards intent on destroying material aspects of "old culture" (Branigan 2008).

Despite this SACH emphasis on culture and nature, not religion and history, UNESCO evaluators and Chinese state authorities agreed on the main threat to Wutai: tourism. For example, the *Nomination Report* cites uncontrolled tourism as the primary danger to preservation:

> The largest threats to the physical conditions of the temples and ancient buildings lie with unauthorized constructions of tourist service facilities

> in the surrounding area of the Taihuai Proposed Core Zone, which have seriously marred the historical and environmental integrity as well as the religious ambience. (GOC 2008b:228)

Moreover, the report argues, the road system was not "rational," local residents were much more interested in making money from tourism than helping protect temples from tourists, and too much parking was available, which encouraged more people to drive to the area (233–234).

The solution to this perceived threat was precisely what UNESCO advocates: spatial segregation. Shortly after Wutai Shan became a national park in 2005, provincial authorities issued a revised master plan that divided the approximately 250 square miles of the new park into four zones: a "strict resource conservation zone," a "controlled resource utilization zone," a "service facility development zone," and a "periphery protection zone" (GOC 2008b:240–241). All of Taihuai town along with the Foguang Temple was included in the core conservation zone. Within these areas, construction that threatened the "authenticity of cultural resources" (GOC 2008a:211) was not allowed. To protect these areas, the plan called for the removal of 417 households with 1,309 residents from the Taihuai area, including all residents of six villages (Taihuai, Yanglin, Taipingjie, Yingfang, Wayao, and Xigou), as well as parts of two others (Dongzhuang and Guizicun). These residents were to be resettled in a new planned community near the south entrance to the park. In addition, 36 guesthouses and 108 shops will be demolished in the core zone and tourist facilities relocated to a new service complex, also near the south gate (288).

This relocation of local residents from the core zone to the park borders will, however, benefit local residents, according to planners. Within what is referred to as a "landscape controlled community" preservation will, the authors assert, spur development: "Under the principle of protecting natural and cultural resources, certain restrictions and guidance are given for community production and living, which may drive healthy social and economic development in the community" (GOC 2008a:215). This will increase local education levels, which would lead residents to recognize the value of cultural heritage, become supporters of heritage conservation, and accept a change of life (Figure 3.1).

This master plan for the management of Wutai Shan as a world heritage site is based on implementing a policy of functional and spatial segregation, just as UNESCO advocates. This approach conceives of a heritage site as a series of zones, ranging from a culturally "pure" inner core of preservation to an "impure" outer zone of commerce and local life. As noted in Chapter I, this planning vision is the product of a particular aesthetic perspective, one rooted in the High Modernist ideals

Figure 3.1 How the master plan envisions displacement: 1,857 new housing units for 6,500 residents to be built at Jingangku village, near the south gate of Wutai National Park.

of the mid-twentieth century that embraced functional segregation as a foundational organizational principle (cf. Scott, 1998). Its roots, however, are found in the early preservation and conservation movements in the United States. Though preservationists and conservationists differ over how protected lands should be managed, they implicitly agree on one fundamental point: these sites should not have permanent inhabitants.

This is no doubt self-evident to most Americans and Europeans: of course people do not live in parks. Nevertheless, this is a culturally embedded value judgment, one which differs significantly from how the categories of culture and nature were conceptualized in Chinese society before communism and, by implication, the value placed on material authenticity.

As seen in the late nineteenth century debates in the United States about the purpose of national parks and forest preserves, discussions about the environment typically focus on use versus protection and conservation versus preservation. That is, most arguments center on the extent to which people should exploit, preserve, and manage natural areas. Each of these perspectives assumes a nature/culture divide, which in turn assumes that humans act upon a space called nature. Nature, often conflated with the environment, is taken to exist elsewhere, not within society, and its value rests on the fact that it has not been utilized by humans. As one philosopher of the environment puts this: "We value the forest and river in part because they are representative of the world outside our dominion, because their existence is independent of us" (Elliot 1995:82). In other words, the ontology of a space is presumed to determine its relative value. Thus a primeval forest is more natural and hence more valuable than a regrowth forest because it has not been acted upon by humans. Humans from this perspective are situated outside of nature.

As a consequence, a hallmark of modernity is accepting as a given not just the need for nature preserves and parks, but more importantly the ideal form of these, places that have as little permanent human presence as possible. We thus go back to nature when we visit, say, Yosemite or the Grand Canyon (although what we find in these places are many people like us, seeking something called nature).

While a natural space cleansed of a permanent human presence might seem second nature to many Americans, this environmental perspective is far from universal. Nature in Chinese, *zi ran*, translates as "all reality becoming" as part of the five elements (fire, water, earth, wood, and metal), conveying a sense of self-evident spontaneity (Li and Sofield 2009:159). Nature, in this sense, just *is*: all reality, everything, or as Daoists would say, the "just-so." This Chinese sense of nature is crucially different from a Euro-American sense in one key aspect: it does not denote either an essential quality or an otherworldly force that directs reality, both of which are core meanings of the English word "nature" (Weller 2006:21). Thus, to say in Chinese that a product is "all natural" or that an event was an "act of nature" is much more difficult, simply because humans from a Chinese linguistic perspective are part of nature, too. For example, a food product defined as all natural in English means that it has not been sullied by human inputs (a linguistic sleight of hand, given that someone had to have produced or grown it). Yet calling such a product *ziran* makes no sense.

Similarly, the ambiguity of the term "wilderness" in the Euro-American tradition is noticeably absent in Chinese. Both historically and linguistically, the center (*zhong*) has been characterized by its possession of civilization and culture, while the periphery is not different because it is closer to nature but because it is uncivilized. Nature is part and parcel of this civilized sphere, not its opposite. Rather than being located outside nature, humans from both a Confucian and Daoist perspective exist within a web of mutual dependency with the world around them. For example, in the *Analects* Confucius speaks of the happiness men who cultivate their humaneness (*ren*) find in mountains (VI.23) while Laozi asserted that "the ways of men are conditioned by those of earth, the ways of earth by those of heaven, the ways of heaven by those of Dao, and the ways of Dao by self so" (Laozi 1999:51). This anthropocosmic perspective links people with past and present in an (ideally) harmonious mutual dependence premised on a desire to tame and control not nature but *qi*, the energy force that emanates everywhere, as a means of both personal improvement and social order (Weller 2006:23–29). Nature and the natural world in this sense are characterized by the pervasiveness of *qi*, the lack of any division between humans and the physical world, and an obligation for humans to use the physical world to benefit themselves and others. Nature exists within a shared landscape, one that is neither a detached space for contemplation or objective enquiry nor the opposite of culture.

This can be seen in what remains even today a common Chinese artistic form, *shanshui* (mountain and water) landscape paintings, an artistic style developed in the late fifth century CE. These paintings are not celebrations of wilderness or an abstract nature as are, for example, nineteenth-century paintings of the Romantic style. Instead, *shanshui* paintings evoke a *cultivated* nature, one in which humans are firmly present (Han 2006:25). This is why human forms are typically present in *shanshui* paintings, along with evidence of civilization such as temples, pavilions, and poetry. Together, these elements (mountains, water, built space, writing, and people) constitute the "just-so" of reality.

Similarly, travel as an exercise in experiential learning and enjoyment has been a foundational part of the Chinese worldview since at least Confucius. The roots of the Chinese term for travel (*luyou*) are not in physical exertion and work (*travail*) as in Romance languages but in fun, companionship, and entertainment (Han 2006:83). Indeed, wandering has been a hallmark of intellectual enquiry in China for more than two millennia. Confucius, as well as the legendary figure Laozi, is reputed to have spent much of their adult lives wandering, while Buddhism reached East Asia with Indian monks traveling along the Silk Road. The importance of travel in the Chinese worldview still resonates in the present as seen, for example, with the place of the Long March in popular culture. Covering 8,000 miles between October 1934 and October 1935, this journey by communist forces from Jiangxi to Shaanxi Provinces remains a seminal event in the history of the Chinese Communist Party. During the initial period of the Cultural Revolution, millions of high school and college students set off on trips around the country to visit revolutionary sites such as Shaoshan, Hunan (Mao's birthplace), Yan'an, Shaanxi (the *de facto* capital of the CCP from 1936 until 1948), and various destinations along the route of the Long March. This mass movement of youth in the name of "exchanging experiences" (*chuan lien*) culminated with enormous rallies in Beijing's Tiananmen Square in November 1966 attended by 2.5 million Red Guards ("Chairman Mao Reviews" 1966).

Of course, this anthropocosmic view of the relationship of humans with the material reality of the world can serve as the basis for not just a social order that uses the physical world. It can also provide a rationale for the subjugation of nature as seen, for example, during the Maoist era in China when state-directed campaigns to transcend Marxist historical stages led to widespread deforestation, flooding, famine, and the forced resettlement of millions of people. But Maoism alone is not to blame. The modernization movement in China did not begin with the Communist Party or with Mao but with late- nineteenth-century Qing efforts to build a modern regime, using as a model Meiji Japan. The exploitation of natural resources and reworking of landscapes has been enthusiastically supported by, in turn, Qing reformers, Chinese Nationalists, and the Communist Party. This approach, which culminated with Mao's campaigns to conquer both nature and history during first the Great Leap Forward and then the Cultural Revolution, was just as much an outgrowth of a Confucian emphasis on controlling nature as it was a rejection of Confucianism. What Mao rejected was not Confucian views of nature per se, but the Confucian emphasis on using nature within an overarching structure of harmony. Confucian utility and harmony (the harmony of heaven and people, *tian ren heyi*) were replaced by Maoist utopianism and conquest (Shapiro 2001:7). As a peasant-based party, the CCP at this period thus took a seemingly contradictory yet logical approach to nature: it was to be used in the service of revolutionary progress yet also was to be the cure for the bourgeois decadence of urban life (Weller 2006:59). For example, during the 1957 anti-Rightist Movement, hundreds of thousands of urban intellectuals and students were purged and exiled to rural labor camps in the frontier regions of Xinjiang, Qinghai, and Manchuria for suspected political disloyalty. Later, in 1968, Mao launched the Down to the Countryside Movement (*shangshan xiacun yundong*), which over the next decade led to the forced resettlement of as many as eighteen million urban youth in rural villages, where they were supposed to learn from peasants and thereby become better revolutionaries and citizens.

This strange mix of Enlightenment authoritarianism, neo-Confucianism, and peasant Romanticism as a foundation for contemporary Chinese views of nature and culture is further complicated by Buddhism. For example, Buddhism's emphasis on the transience of reality raises practical questions about the underlying utility of preservation (an idealized material permanence). This does not mean that monastic communities cannot possess wealth, if its purpose is to support devotion (Kieschnick

2003:6). In fact, after the late Tang Dynasty attacks on Buddhism in 845 CE, the accumulation of material objects and wealth by monasteries and temples was never widely condemned in China until the nationalist and communist political movements in the early twentieth century. Strict preservation of material objects, however, has not been a priority of monastic authorities, as illustrated by the shared Buddhist and Confucian acceptance of temple renewal (*weixin*). This concept of temple renewal, which in Chinese implies revitalization *and* modernization, illustrates how Chinese philosophy and religious practice do not have a culturally embedded suspicion of cultural change, either tangible or intangible (Zhang et al. 1997:78).

Foguang Temple, located outside the Wutai valley, is an example of this dynamic process of change and transition. Originally built between 471 and 499 during the Northern Wei dynasty, it was expanded at the end of the Sui (581–618) and in the early Tang (618–907) dynasties. After being completely rebuilt in 633, a three-story pavilion was added in 820. In 845, the complex was destroyed during the anti-Buddhist campaign by Emperor Wuzong and then was rebuilt between 847 and 860. During the Jin Dynasty (1115–1234), two new halls (Manjusri and Visyabhadra) were added, and in the early twelfth century, these two halls, along with a third hall (Devajara) were completely rebuilt. Major renovations of the entire complex were later carried out during both the Ming (1368–1644) and Qing (1644–1911) dynasties. This complex history of material renewal is flattened out, however, by preservationists, who emphasize the Tang Dynasty-era elements of this site. The Global Heritage Fund, for example, asserts that the complex was built in the Tang Dynasty but then "forgotten for centuries" and only rediscovered in 1937 (GHF 2009).

Foguang is not a unique case. Bishan temple, one of the eight listed world heritage sites around Taihuai, was also constructed in the fifth century. Over the course of time, it disappeared as a built space, becoming instead a collection of cave dwellings for monk recluses. However, the temple was rebuilt during the Ming Dynasty in 1525. After the Manchurian conquest of China and establishment of the Qing Dynasty, it was extensively renovated in 1692, 1818 and 1906. It was further rebuilt again in 1913, after the Republic was established (UNESCO 2009:2). What precise layers of this built, destroyed, transformed, rebuilt, renovated and renewed and revitalized tangible space qualify as heritage? And, if all do, given this historical record of layering, why then assume that declaring this temple a heritage site should require an end to this historical process of continuous change?

Given the syncretic context of Buddhist material culture and the lack of emphasis in Chinese culture on tangible cultural preservation, how to justify a prescriptive approach that is premised on just such a cultural assumption? From a UNESCO perspective, protecting the authenticity of a heritage site requires strict adherence to the material integrity of both cultural and natural sites. As a formality, the master plan accepts this interpretation. For example, it highlights the goal of preserving the original "form, design, material and functions" of temples and monasteries (GOC 2008b:236–237), rejects the reconstruction of disappeared heritage and asserts that "new construction, expansion and renovation are prohibited" (239). The authors concede that a number of the temples in the core zone have been significantly renovated over the centuries, which could call into question the integrity of their authenticity, if this is defined in strict preservationist terms. However, they argue that these sites are indeed authentic for two reasons: first, "the overall arrangement of the majority of buildings is identical to the time they were built" (212) and second, the function of these buildings as religious worship sites has not changed (215). Ironically, from this cultural and aesthetic perspective, the transformation of these temples into world heritage destinations for global visitors would actually *decrease* their authenticity because this process would transform their primary purpose into museum display, not religious practice.

Nevertheless, the UNESCO approach to the organization of heritage space, which spatially separates heritage sites, nature preserves, and public parks from the built space of existing human communities, has become a global hegemonic model. Under the auspices of UNESCO, it serves as a transnational blueprint for how both natural and cultural sites should be defined, framed, and cared for in relation to existing communities. This, then, is the paradox of preservation: UNESCO seeks to preserve the cultural diversity of the world in an era of globalization which is presumed to carry the eminent threat of cultural sameness, yet in doing so it mandates a specific spatial form of preservation that erases cultural differences and evokes and promotes the cultural sameness it fears.

In the case of Wutai Shan and other heritage sites that have witnessed the displacement of local residents in China, critics of the Chinese government thus have their facts wrong. People are not displaced only because of government policies that remove residents in the name of economic development (as often is the case in urban China) or because the government and Party are antireligious but because relevant government authorities faithfully adhere to UNESCO guidelines on what makes a place a world heritage site. In doing so, they contribute to an ongoing erasure of cultural differences by transforming places such as Wutai Shan into generic examples of world heritage where preserved space comes to look like heritage space everywhere.

However, preserving Wutai Shan as an example of the world's heritage is not the main impetus behind these policies. Instead, what has occurred in the name of preservation is closely connected to the Communist Party's attention to the moral and spiritual aspects of modernization, as discussed in Chapter II. In this regard, the framing, codifying, and presentation of Wutai Shan as a world heritage site is aimed at two key audiences, domestic tourists and local residents, not at international visitors.

THE LANGUAGE OF HERITAGE

Most visitors to Wutai Shan arrive at the south gate of the new national park. After paying an admission fee of 168 yuan and a transportation fee of 50 yuan, visitors travel approximately twelve kilometers pass rice fields, several small villages, and the new planned community of Jinggangku before reaching the core heritage zone. This is marked not by another gate but by a large signboard in the form of a wall built to look heritage like (Figure 3.2). This depicts a map of the valley and provides a synopsis of the official narrative.

Figure 3.2 Introduction to Wutai Shan National Park, near the south entrance of the park.

Echoing the language of the original nomination of Wutai Shan for world heritage status, this narrative is as much about the geography of Wutai Shan and its scientific value as it is about the historical importance of the valley as a Buddhist pilgrimage site. Written only in Chinese, it makes no attempt to speak to an international audience.

> WORLD HERITAGE: MOUNT WUTAI
>
> Mount Wutai, home to Wenshu Bodhisattva, is one of the most famous Buddhist mountains in China. It was inscribed as one of the first State Level Scenic Spots in 1982, as a National Park in 1992, as a National Geology Park in 2004, as a "Chinese AAAAA Tourism Area" in 2007, and as a UNESCO World Heritage Site in 2009. Mount Wutai is famous for its five rounded peaks: North, South, East, West, and Central. The North Peak, the highest mountain in North China, reaches an altitude of 3061.1 meters. Wutai National Park consists of 599 square kilometers of scenery and famous sites and is one of the Four Sacred Mountains in Chinese Buddhism. It is also viewed as one of the greatest places in the world for Buddhism practice. There are many Buddhist statues, wall-paintings, and classics to see, and music to hear. Mount Wutai also has geological data from the meso-archaeozoic to the paleo-proterozic periods, which proves the evolution of the earth. Buddhism and the beautiful mountain scenery create a perfect mixture, which mirrors the harmonious coexistence of people and nature.

A similar message is delivered by a Chinese language billboard hanging on the outside wall of the Pushou Temple in Taihuai (Figure 3.3). Beneath UNESCO and World Heritage emblems, an explanation of world heritage is provided. This is followed by the official narrative of Wutai Shan: its status as one of China's four Buddhist mountains, one of the world's five most important Buddhist places, and a national scenic destination; its listing as, among other categories, a national forest preserve, a national cultural relic, and a famous scenic spot; and finally its fame as a "national five star tourist scenic area." "Wutai Shan truly is an outstanding and valuable contribution to the world," this sign declares. A synopsis of the world heritage nomination and acceptance process completes this narrative.

On the right side of this signboard, however, a very different narrative is provided. This displays the Wutai Shan scenic area "civilized rules" (*wenming shouze*) of behavior. These include "four nos" and "six wants," standards to meet and rules to observe. These rules are certainly not aimed at foreign visitors (since they are written in Chinese). Nor are these aimed at Chinese visitors. Instead, the target audience is local residents. Scenic area residents, these rules declare, must not spit, write

Figure 3.3 Wutai's world heritage fame and rules of behavior. These are written exclusively in Chinese and aimed at local residents, not visitors.

graffiti, litter, use coarse or foul language, damage public property, or vend without a license.

These rules of public etiquette echo long-standing Communist Party attempts to change what it perceives to be backward and uncivilized behavior associated with peasants. They also to a remarkable degree echo the goals of the Nationalist Party's New Life Movement of 1934–1938. This emphasis on exhorting local residents to act civilized in public illustrates the educational basis of heritage in China. This is not, however, merely an educational campaign about the past. The objective is not for residents only to become knowledgeable about the history of Wutai but to become cultured through repetitive interactions with more modern and hence civilized people, tourists from more developed and hence more modern places in China. These prohibitions establish a foundation for this ideal interaction by stating what local residents should not do. People first must wipe their hearts and minds of existing social norms in order to be open to learning. Visitors are therefore not simply tourists but models of proper behavior. Consciously or not, they are charged with showing local residents how to become modern Chinese subjects.

The "Six Rules of Civilized Behavior" sketch out how residents can become more civilized:

1. Be patriotic, love your country, take care of your health, and build a successful scenic area.
2. Be polite, act civilized, love your work, and be honest.
3. Cultivate a harmonious family, respect the old and care for the young, follow the one child policy, and don't be wasteful.
4. Respect education, respect scientific knowledge, be friendly, and help others.
5. Take care of public property, keep this place clean, plant trees, and make the environment [the scenery] beautiful.
6. Follow and obey the law, report illegal activity, eradicate superstition, and do not gamble.

Patriotism, personal health, civilized behavior, hard work, adherence to state policies on family planning, and a clean and healthy environment are presented as everyday standards to live by. Like caring for the old and the young, having a stable family, and helping those in need, these are virtues commonly depicted in Chinese television dramas and series, movies, and news stories. Together, they encapsulate the reconstituted Confucian ethical basis of contemporary government social policies and reflect a state emphasis on a moral framework that has been gutted of Maoist ideology.

However, the fourth and sixth rules are more perplexing. Respecting scientific knowledge and eradicating superstition are political slogans that have been staples of the Communist Party's public message since its establishment nearly a century ago and reflect a core Marxist belief about the role, or rather lack thereof, of religion in society. Following Liberation in 1949, the Party asserted control over not just religious practice but also a wide range of cultivation practices associated with *weisheng* (preserving life) and *qi* (the vital energy source) that date back to the Zhou Dynasty (ninth century BCE). Over the following three thousand years, Confucianism, Daoism, Tibetan, Chan, and Mahayana schools of Buddhism, medical practitioners and various forms of martial arts developed cultivation practices that are often lumped together under the category of qigong (Xu 1999:966–967). Faced with such a widespread belief in the efficacy of *qi* practices, Party authorities classified some of these practices as scientific and medical and others as superstitions (*mixin*, blind following of the heart). Practices that could be classified within the scientific paradigm (and hence not forms of blind belief or superstition) were allowed under strict state regulation, while other, nonscientific practices were banned on the basis of their backward characteristics (Xu 1999:976–82). Practicing and promoting superstitions was a common charge against religious believers during much of the post-1949 era and was the basis for the banning of the Falun Gong movement in April 1999 (Chang 2004).

This ongoing public critique of superstition illustrates the tension between an idealized Party and State view of how citizens should think and the cultural and social realities of contemporary Chinese society. Of course, what counts as feudal and superstitious is not fixed, as seen for example in the contemporary toleration of religious practice through State-sanctioned and controlled Christian, Buddhist, and Muslim associations. What has been a constant since 1949 is the insistence on the part of the Party that it has the authority to determine what constitutes "superstition" at specific historical moments (Anagnost 1994:234). Thus the location of this signboard in front of a recently built (and state sanctioned and supported) Buddhist Studies Institute is, from a Party perspective, perfectly logical.

Nevertheless, how are residents supposed to overcome superstitions and embrace the logical positivism of science when the subject matter of Wutai Shan's world heritage status, reverence to Buddha [*baifo*] is from a Communist Party perspective a form of superstition? The Party solution is to redefine Wutai Shan as a world heritage site of culture, not Buddhism, and emphasize for local residents the cultivation of modern virtues, not Buddhist virtues and ethics.

A similar message is supposed to be provided by tour guides. All tour guides in China are state licensed. This means for someone to work as a guide she must pass a battery of fact-based tests. The subject matter of these tests is very similar to the information collected in geographic gazetteers, which have a long history in China dating back to the Han Dynasty. During the Ming and Qing eras, thousands of gazetteers were produced for different areas. These usually included listings of local scenic spots, provided poems and quotes associated with these, named local mountains, rivers, and temples, and described local foods, delicacies, eminent families, and myths and legends (Nyíri 2006a). Today's state-licensed guides in essence function as living embodiments of these combination geographic handbooks, tour books, and historical atlases.

At Wutai Shan, as at other scenic spots in China, tour guides serve as a reference point for the official narrative of this site, fleshing out the factual bullet points visitors are provided on signboards and billboards (Figure 3.4). Guiding is also highly gendered; the overwhelming majority of local guides are women between the ages of twenty-two and twenty-five. They are a common sight during the tourist season that runs from late spring until the October holidays. Typically carrying a battery

Figure 3.4 A tour guide at work, Taihuai. Most guides are young women with little actual knowledge of Buddhism.

powered megaphone and waving a small pennant that identifies their company, they always wear a large identity badge around their necks. This not only gains them entry to temples and other tourist sites, it also marks them as professionals to their audience.

Market reforms have impacted the tourism business in China as much as other state-controlled industries. With the hollowing out of socialist employment guarantees, guiding is no longer the prestigious (and materially secure) job it was in an earlier era. Instead, especially at the local level and in marginal places such as Shanxi province guiding has become a seasonal occupation for the young. During winter months when tourism at Wutai Shan stops, some guides with connections are able to find work leading tour groups from the provincial cities of Taiyuan and Datong to southern destinations such as Guangzhou and Hainan Island. But most have to survive on their summer earnings. These in turn are heavily influenced by tips because salaries are quite low. This need to entertain and please their audience to boost their earnings in turn influences how guides manage and present the official state narrative of Wutai Shan. Much like in the mass media industry in China, the outcome of this shifting landscape is not a pure and unadulterated space of free speech but a more complex message, one which informs the audience and offers a multiperspective narrative but in a way that does not openly contest the official story. So in the case of Wutai

Shan, successful guides do not frame this site merely as a storehouse of Chinese culture and history, a world heritage site for Buddhists, and a geological landscape of unique rocks and fauna. They instead describe Wutai Shan as a place of Buddhist charismatic power and authority but in the language of an observer, not a believer. In the following narrative, the speaker, a twenty-seven-year-old local guide, leads a group of tourists from Tianjin through the Xiantong and Tayuan temples. Her monologue shifts between empirical facts (the White Pagoda is 56.37 meters high and is painted with a crushed limestone paste), legends and half-truths (monks have magical powers to fight evil and do good), a primer on Buddhism (we should seek to overcome our personal desires), and pointers on how to worship (follow pilgrims clockwise, turn prayer wheels, burn incense, and chant). But she also evokes scientific authority (cameras do not lie) to prove the magical (a yellow light emanating from the top of the White Pagoda is evidence of the presence of Buddha). The narrative that results does not reject the official story but instead returns the sacred, mystical, and magical to this, not as a counterpoint but as a complement:

> Inside this temple people come to seek Buddha's protection. In the main hall on the left there is a table, on that you can write your wishes. Write down your full names and the masters will pray for your good fortunes every morning. That's what they do. They get up very early every morning to pray for people. That's how this temple works. Come closer to listen please; come forward in the main hall and circle clockwise, walk to the left. Don't you feel awed by this? That one there is a very special Bodhisattva, Manjusri [*Wenshu Pusa*]. If you want to burn incense here go and talk to the vendors, they can sell you some.

After this brief introduction, she led her group into the main hall, where she gathered them in front of a small table.

> This entire floor was originally made of jade. Do you believe me? This is what the monks claim. If a person can only experience one thing in this world, it should be a place like this. Isn't it so beautiful? Buddhism says this is the way the world is: people always have desires and they want what they want, so to overcome these wants they should call on the Buddha of Light, Amit bha [*Ahmituo*], the Bodhisattva of Wisdom, Manjusri, and the Bodhisattva of Meditation, Samantabhadra [*Puxian Pusa*]. This is what you are looking at now: Amit bha in the center, Manjusri on the left and Samantabhadra on the right. See the people worshipping? This is a very important place for people to worship Buddha [*baifo*]. If you look below the Buddha you can see a photograph. This photograph

> is from June 1, 2009, the date when a Buddhist council was held here at Tayuan. A great many masters gathered together for this special meeting. During the meeting some of the monks discovered that the top of the Pagoda was shining. Now this photograph is evidence. It shows at the very top of the pagoda a yellow light, and in this light is an image of Buddha. See? Look at the light and at Buddha. Go ahead and take a photograph [of the photo] but be careful! When we are at a site such as this we should all pay our respects.

The group moved outside and continued on to the inner courtyard of Tayuan Temple, where her description shifted from arguing for the empirically proven validity of a Buddhist aura (cameras do not lie) to a materialist description of the White Pagoda, speculation about what it might contain, and a reminder of the magical power monks could supposedly evoke to fight evil:

> Here we are at the Great White Pagoda. It was built in the fifth year of the Yuan Dynasty, 1301, so is more than 700 years old. It is 56.37 meters high, equivalent to a nine storey building. It is as solid now as when it was built because they knew advanced architectural principles. It is constructed of bricks and is covered with white paint made from limestone. Limestone is crushed and mixed with water and made into a paste. When applied it makes the surface look like stone. Does anyone know the reason why? When this pagoda was built each brick was fitted exactly together with precise measurements and covered, and it was just as strong as if it were stone. In 2004 the white pagoda was repainted at a cost of one million yuan because this is a national and world heritage site. Just look at how big it is! In the center is an underground palace containing Buddhist relics [bones]. What exactly is in there we cannot say because it cannot be opened, but besides relics, there are the five metals (gold, silver, copper, iron and tin) as well as statues. At Xian just such an underground palace was opened up 87 years ago and excavated by archeologists. Buddhists say that seeing Buddhist relics is just like seeing Buddha, and worshipping a relic is the same as worshipping a Bodhisattva . . . we cannot climb on top of the pagoda but we can circle it, just like the pilgrims are doing, and turn the prayer wheels. You notice they also chant as they do this, like this: "Goddess of Mercy [*Guanyin Pusa*], ohm mani padmi ohm." How many of you have seen the television drama, "Monk"? You've seen it, right? They [monks] have magic powers. When they want to use these powers they chant "ohm mani padmi ohm" and then they can fight evil and do good. So you all should try chanting to Guanyin, but slowly, and make sure you feel this in your heart. This way you receive her protection.

CONCLUSION

From a preservationist perspective, the removal of residents from around buildings that are considered to be priceless because of their historical and aesthetic attributes is, strictly speaking, a technical issue. Yet, in promoting technical issues of preservation and management issues of conservation within a spatial framework of functional segregation, UNESCO and ICOMOS ignore the political and social impact heritage projects such as the Wutai Shan National Park have on local residents. Although the authors of the *Conversation and Management Plan for the Nominated World Heritage Site of Mount Wutai* allude to local partnership and a "multi-stakeholder partnership," these are defined as collaboration between different levels of government, not with local residents. The latter are assumed to be represented by local government officials (GOC 2008a:207). Thus, "community partnership and development" is presented as an unqualified good, since this will lead local residents to "improve or change their way of life and production to minimize the pressure on conservation of heritage sites" and to "gain a better understanding of the value of cultural heritage and strengthen their awareness of heritage conservation" (207–208).

As previously noted, heritage (*yichan*) is a quite new concept in Chinese, coined by state authorities in the Deng-era economic reform period. Heritage sites are consequently also quite new. Until the state promotion of Wutai Shan as a heritage site began in the early 1990s, local residents did not think of themselves as inhabiting a heritage site but instead a pilgrimage destination. The recognition and promotion of heritage in Taihuai has meant in practice the dispossession of local people. This is because local culture, in the sense of the lived experiences of local people, is considered to have no value. What has value is the material culture of Buddhism. For UNESCO and the Chinese Communist Party, these buildings and temples are worthy of special status because they are first of all historical, not religious.

There are, however, key differences between the UNESCO view of Wutai Shan and the local governmental view. For example, the master plan advocates not just "rectification and relocation" policies to protect temples within the core zone but also tour guide training and the promotion of the heritage zone as a national tourism destination (GOC 2008b:186). In other words, while local planners share UNESCO concerns about unchecked economic development, where the two sides differ is in the role of tourism. For UNESCO, tourism, particularly mass tourism, is invariably a potential threat, whereas this document cites "scientific tourism" as beneficial because this will generate revenue and provide the public with "opportunities for training and education" as well as a better appreciation of world heritage (198). Tourism, in other words, will provide local economic opportunities and contribute to the ongoing national campaign to increase the quality of citizens through improving the overall civility of Chinese society.

In practice, and perhaps quite predictably, few local residents voice concerns about cultural heritage. They instead focus on how this state project impacts their own lives. Heritage preservation in this case has meant the displacement of residents, the widespread destruction of homes and other buildings, and the construction of a range of visitor facilities. The ways in which local residents react to these policies is the subject of Chapter IV.

Chapter IV

Heritage from Below

Displacement, Construction, and Reconstruction

The character 拆 (*chai*), which translates as "to dismantle or tear down," has become a common sight in Chinese urban neighborhoods targeted for economic development projects. Painted in white on the side of buildings and walls, it graphically marks the profound shift in the Chinese Communist Party's development objectives since Deng Xiaoping proclaimed his policy of "reform and opening" in 1978, encouraged private capital investment and began dismantling the socialist aspects of the state. After 1949, the new government had encouraged and led a wholesale rejection of China's feudal past and the quasi-capitalism practiced by the defeated nationalists. In their place, it substituted social and economic equality, rapid industrialization, and world revolutionary socialism. For the next three decades, citizens endured national political campaigns against "bad elements" and "bourgeois revisionists", and themselves suffered arrest, imprisonment, or worse if identified as such. At the same time, the new regime reworked the relationship between people, built space, and land, organizing urban dwellers into work units and peasants into collectives and eventually communes. As noted in Chapter II, the political and moral objective of this massive reorganization of society was the development of a new type of citizen, one who transcended familial and clan ties and identified with the Party-State and socialism.

In contemporary China, much of the built living space of this socialist period has been privatized, corporatized, or erased. Public housing complexes and entire work units in strategically located urban neighborhoods have been demolished to make way for highways, shopping centers, office buildings, and luxury apartment complexes, while in rural

Faith in Heritage: Displacement, Development, and Religious Tourism in Contemporary China by Robert J. Shepherd, 91–120

areas near booming cities local authorities have turned farm land over to real estate developers. This whirlwind process of creative destruction has been widely reported in the Chinese media and on Internet blogs and has led to the coinage of a new term, "nail house" (*dīngzihù*) to describe residents who refuse to move when confronted by development projects, citing inadequate compensation.

Conflicts over compensation rates and a widespread perception that local authorities usually support the interests of real estate developers has fueled this coverage and has led the central government to try to impose more transparency and fairness on the (re)development process. Moreover, media coverage has increased awareness of legal rights among both urban and rural residents, leading more people to resist initial compensation offers.

What makes Wutai Shan unusual in this story of displacement in the name of development is that residents and businesses are not being removed to make way for another shopping mall, golf course, or new condominium complex but for heritage preservation. In other words, people have been told they must move to preserve and promote, ironically, material examples of the very feudal past the Chinese Communist Party promised to abolish when it seized power in 1949. Whereas Chinese citizens in the recent past were urged by the CCP to sacrifice the present for a future of world revolutionary socialism, local residents of Wutai Shan are now told they must sacrifice *their* present for world heritage. The response has been not open resistance but a series of tactics, beginning with a failed petition to Beijing and culminating in, ironically, a recent burst of new construction. Guesthouses and shops have been built, restaurants and houses renovated and expanded, and utilities and other fixtures added. On the surface, these investments do not seem logical, at least from a theoretical economic perspective. Why would a business owner invest in a building that will soon be demolished? Why is such construction happening under a cloud of almost-certain destruction?

Another, more understandable, building boom is unfolding among religious institutions. For monasteries and temples, being categorized as a heritage site to be preserved has meant an opportunity to renovate, expand, and in some cases create entirely new "heritage" spaces. It has also led to new sources of revenue. Indeed, far from being transformed into preserved and frozen museum-like sites, the most popular temples and monasteries have become dynamic sources of religious aspiration, learning, and wealth. The net result is not a unified community response to the master plan for transforming Wutai Shan in general and Taihuai in particular into a new form of built space. Instead, this plan has created new opportunities for some monastic communities and local residents while harming others.

Finally, a third construction boom is also ongoing outside the core zone of Taihuai. A few kilometers inside the south gate of Wutai National Park, state authorities have spent millions of dollars constructing a new community for residents displaced from Taihuai along with a visitor complex consisting of a museum, shopping complex, and convention center. Next to this tourism complex, a private developer is building a gated mountain resort containing a five-star hotel, luxury townhouses, and an artificial lake. All of this construction is occurring on appropriated farmland. This illustrates the emergence of a new form of property relationship in China, one in which built space is privately owned and yet all land remains the property of the state.

I begin with a brief review of this process before turning to how privatization, increased party and state tolerance of religious practice, and a central government directive for local authorities to promote economic development have all contributed to a complex web of destruction, construction, and reconstruction of heritage at Wutai Shan.

The Privatization of Real Estate

The primary objective of the economic and social reforms begun by Deng Xiaoping is the rapid modernization of China. Deng explicitly delinked politics from economic development policies, thereby seeking to assure foreign investors and Chinese citizens that the realm of market action would no longer be subject to ideological benchmarks. Consequently, national authorities concentrated on reforming private property law, not civil law, first. In effect, the CCP under the direction of Deng offered a new social contract to people in the wake of Maoism: Chinese citizens could own property, accumulate wealth, and enjoy increased personal autonomy as long as they did not challenge the political authority of the Party.

At the time of Mao's death in 1976, almost all urban residents lived in state-controlled housing organized as work units, and peasants usually lived in their own houses but were organized into cooperatives and communes. Housing reforms in urban areas began with an experimental program in Xian and Nanjing in 1979 to construct and sell new housing at cost. This policy failed for the simple reason that few people had enough savings to buy these units, even at cost (Zhang 1998:134). A subsidized program was next tried in Zhejiang and Hubei Provinces in 1981 and 1982. Under this program, new housing stock was jointly funded by the central government, work units, and individual occupants, with each contributing one-third of construction cost (Gu and Shen 2003:108). The success of this program led to its expansion to approximately three hundred cities by 1986, including Beijing (Lee 1988:403). However, for these policies to be effective, state officials had to also revise land policies. In 1988, ownership of land was legally separated from use-rights, the former remaining in the hands of the state and the latter granted to individuals. This law was further revised in 1990 to allow anyone who held use-rights to transfer or sell these (Fang and Zhang 2003:150).

These initial reforms focused on increasing the supply of housing not through privatization but through what the government termed "commoditization," in which private citizens became co-owners of their apartments with their work units and central state ministries. This program enabled urban residents without access to subsidized housing to gain use-rights to new housing in exchange for one-third of the construction costs. From the work unit administrative perspective, new apartment blocks could be built quite cheaply because individuals and the government provided two-thirds of the construction costs. From the central government perspective, more urban residents gained housing while the state role in supplying this was significantly reduced (Zhang 1998:129).

More complicated was how to apply housing reforms to already-existing state housing, most of which was located within state-owned enterprise (SOE) work units. Beginning in the early 1990s, work units transferred use-rights of apartments to their occupants at fixed prices. However, use-rights did not carry full property rights; instead, purchasers shared ownership with their work units. These initial policies failed to attract many buyers for a range of reasons. First, few people had enough savings or high enough wages to make down payments. In addition, in the aftermath of the Cultural Revolution, actually getting people to believe that state and party officials supported private housing was not easy. Finally, for people who already had access to subsidized state housing, there was little incentive to purchase the right to use an apartment at a higher price than what they paid to rent this same apartment. For many people, these policies were viewed as an attempt to force them to pay for what they had already earned as a right (Zhang 1998:130).

In response, the State Council issued a directive in 1994 that formalized three forms of housing. Apartments purchased at market price carried full ownership rights; units purchased at cost price carried a five-year rent/resale restriction; and subsidized units provided occupancy rights but could not be resold (Zhang 1998:139). However, these policies only succeeded to the extent that subsidies were offered, which did not actually privatize state housing but instead replicated the triangular partnership between a work unit's central government organ, the work unit itself, and work unit members found among new housing purchasers.

In 1995, the State Council legalized the construction of commercial housing (*shangpin fang*) for sale at market prices as well as price-controlled housing (*jingji fang*) for lower-middle-class residents

(Bray 2005:174). Finally, in 1998, all state-affiliated enterprises and institutes were prohibited from constructing any further housing, and existing housing was mandated for privatization (Wang et al. 2005:1865).

In rural areas, there was little public housing to privatize because most peasants already lived in their own homes. Moreover, for citizens who were assigned to work units in rural areas, gaining the right to buy an apartment they already occupied was seldom advantageous. Indeed, much like urban housing in economically depressed areas such as China's northeastern rustbelt, there was little private demand for rural work unit housing. Instead, reform policies broke up communes and allocated farmland to individual families on long-term leasehold contracts. In both economically depressed urban areas and rural communities, work unit authorities have been able to shed their responsibilities for maintaining housing stock by turning this over to occupants, who may end up owning an apartment they previously had a right to use and for which there is no resale market. This is in stark contrast to people in desirable urban areas fortunate enough to have had access to housing before state policies mandated the selling off of public housing stock. They were able to buy their apartments at low prices and have since become rich on paper. These people are the recipients of double good fortune. First, they were lucky enough to be born into families with urban residency cards (*hukou*), thus by dint of birth having access to better schools and health care, guaranteed employment, and during the Maoist era, subsidized foodstuffs. Second, they were lucky to have found themselves assigned to work units in major cities and, more important, desirable neighborhoods within these cities.

One example of this is state educational institutions. Through the strategic marketing of language teaching (Chinese to foreign students and English to local fee-paying students), culture (studiously separated from politics), and their campuses as a postsocialist form of a gated community, higher educational institutions in desirable urban areas have not only survived but often thrived in the marketplace. But in doing so, how space is both produced and consumed on campuses has shifted. Responses to these changes are neither uniformly positive nor negative.

Life in the Housing Market

> Economic development has been fast, while peoples' living standards are not very high. You know the word *shiye*? *Shiye* means people with no jobs. There are lots of people who are unemployed, who don't have any money. And then there are the job-waiting youth. Here there are so many. (Female informant, Beijing 2009)

Han Mei Li was born and raised on the campus of a Beijing language college. She came of age during the Cultural Revolution, when schools stopped functioning. After receiving minimal training, she was sent to Hubei province as a teenager to work as a barefoot doctor (a basic health practitioner) and returned to her campus home after the death of Mao in 1976. Her father, who was a senior professor at the time, was one of the first people on campus to go to the United States as an exchange scholar in the early 1980s, soon after Han's mother had died. Like many in his situation at that time, he did not return. Meanwhile, Han had been assigned as an office assistant to a campus department and remained in her parents' apartment. When campus authorities announced the privatization of housing in 1998, she discovered that buying would actually penalize her:

> At the time when apartments could be bought, my father was already in America. They said he couldn't buy because he no longer had a *hukou*. . . . I could have bought for myself, but I didn't want to. I thought it was too troublesome. If I had bought, I only could have gotten a small place. You see, the government has to give me a place. So now I am still in my father's place. But it's not his place, it's a work unit place (*shi danweide*).

For those who did buy in 1998, the benefits on paper have been enormous. Residents were able to buy their apartments for 1,400 yuan a square meter; as of the summer of 2010, the unofficial price had risen to 10,000 yuan a square meter. Han's work unit apartment of 31 square meters is currently worth 310,000 yuan, or approximately $48,000. This is still far cheaper than private developments in this area of Beijing, where new two-bedroom apartments cost as much as 20,000 yuan per square meter. The problem is being able to sell. Though campus staff can own their apartments, selling on the open market is extremely difficult because regulations require them to first offer their flats to other employees. Instead, many people now rent their campus apartments and use the income this generates to buy a second apartment off-campus.

Unlike Ms. Han, Chen Ming did buy when he had a chance and has since prospered. Now forty-nine, he moved with his parents and brother to this campus in 1963, at the age of five. In 1966, schools were closed, and in 1969, his family along with those of other staff and faculty were sent down to the countryside, in Hunan province. He received some schooling after the campus reopened in 1972 but did not graduate from high school. Instead, based on his class background (a peasant grandfather and a worker father), he was able to join the navy, and served four years in Fujian. In 1980, back in Beijing, he searched in vain for a job before using family ties to get hired on campus as an office assistant. He then spent eighteen years sharing a small flat with his parents. In 1998, he qualified for a one-room apartment of twenty square meters, which he purchased for 28,000 yuan, or approximately $3,800. In the next three years, both of his parents passed away, and he inherited their two-room apartment of seventy square meters worth 500,000 yuan. Suddenly flush with property, he also became an attractive commodity on the marriage market and soon had a young wife from Anhui Province and baby daughter. His job remains the same as it was in 1980, his salary quite modest. But he now owns two apartments, one of which he rents to a Japanese man for $250 a month, far more than his monthly salary. Quite predictably, Chen is very enthusiastic about government housing reforms.

A very different view is offered by Linda, a relatively new teacher assigned to an English training center on campus. She was hired in 1999, thus missing out on the privatization of campus apartments by one year. She shares a dormitory room with another single teacher in one of the few apartment buildings school authorities have not privatized. Her rent is twenty yuan a month, approximately three dollars. Linda is on a housing list that is clearly a wish list: *if* someone decided to sell their apartment, and *if* it was her turn, then she could buy it. The chances are almost nonexistent. For state employees of her generation, the commercial housing market (*shangping fang*) is supposed to provide for them. But the market price makes it difficult for most state workers to buy a commercial apartment, even when they participate in a provident fund. Linda's situation is actually better than most new teachers and staff. Because the school has no more housing to allocate, authorities rent a building for them in a suburb twenty kilometers away, from which they must commute. Although she enjoys teaching, she recognizes that unless she marries a relatively wealthy man, her chances of ever owning an apartment in the city are slim. For this she blames not the reforms nor the Party but people she calls "outsiders":

> A lot of people buy very expensive houses in Beijing. They are not local people. They're from other places! They make a lot of money somewhere else, and they buy a lot of housing in Beijing for investment. This should be stopped because they are really buying *hukou* status. It's not fair.

Others also fail to prosper in this hybrid system. Though still called a new teacher by her senior colleagues, Li Ying was hired in 1992 after graduating from Qinghai University with a degree in English. A few years later, she married her college sweetheart, who was officially a resident of Qinghai. This marriage did not give him residency rights in Beijing, but he did not care because, as a freelance artist, he had no work unit affiliation. After being hired, Li Ying had been assigned to a dorm room with another female teacher, but in 1994, her roommate had gone to Japan on a fellowship and decided not to return, so Li's husband moved in with her. Li soon had a baby, and when privatization occurred, the family looked forward to a bigger apartment. But because her husband did not bureaucratically exist, Li only qualified for a small one-bedroom flat, based on her official family of herself and her son. Her husband could become bureaucratically real by purchasing a Beijing residency card, but the price is more than 40,000 yuan, which they cannot afford.

Teachers such as Linda have little sympathy for people in Li's position, arguing she at least has received some form of subsidized housing. Yet people like Li, especially older staff and teachers, do not think school authorities have given them anything. Instead, the ability to buy housing at below-market prices is something they have earned, through their years of work, as one retired worker explain:

> When we came here, this place was nothing, just fields and trees. Now look at it. Who built all of these buildings? Who made this a famous institution? We did. We earned our apartments with our own sweat.

This sentiment is widely shared by older and retired staff and teachers. Far from seeing market reforms as a process that has liberated them from the ties of their work unit, they view the transformation of social relationships on campus with profound ambiguity, as a process that has altered lives in *their* community. As one staff member said, "Now you often meet a lot of new faces, you don't know where they come from." A teacher added: "Many people living here don't know each other. Look in teacher X's building—there are many people who are outsiders. Certainly this is a big problem. This is a capitalist world now, it's like in America." Others were less sanguine:

> Life is so chaotic now! There are Koreans, Americans, Japanese, outsiders (*waidi ren*), students . . . my building is so chaotic . . . even migrants (*mangliu*). If anyone has the money, they can rent. What about security now? And our work unit?

DEVELOPMENT THROUGH DISPLACEMENT

The situation is quite different in Taihuai, in the center of Wutai National Park. As in other rural areas in China, agricultural land was nationalized after 1949 and redistributed to peasant families, including the landholdings of monasteries and temples. However, these populist policies were quickly abandoned and collectives established, followed soon after during the Great Leap Forward by communes. Although no one was allowed to operate private businesses or possess private property, housing in the countryside remained a family responsibility. This meant that recent housing reforms had little initial relevance in rural areas because little public housing stock existed to privatize. Land reforms after 1982 gave collectives the authority to lease land to individual families. Further reforms in 1988 separated land ownership from use-rights and allowed small businesses. Local governments could sign land-use contracts with individuals, who, for a fee, were guaranteed a plot of land for a fixed period of time along with the right to sell use-rights to others. For commercial use, these contracts can be for as long as forty years.

This privatization of land use, not ownership, stimulated the growth of a private small business sector in rural communities, just as it did in urban neighborhoods. In Taihuai, the result was the reemergence of a local market economy centered on religion and tourism. Individuals and families signed contracts with local authorities for land plots in town and built shops, restaurants, and hostels that catered to visitors, monks, and nuns. The built space of the town is consequently relatively new, with few buildings dating before the late eighties. Until plans were finalized for the removal of residents, most of these buildings were one or two stories and made of cheap local bricks covered with a cement finish. Moreover, not all families that run businesses in the town are actually from Taihuai. Besides people from the local area, there are shopkeepers from Datong and Taiyuan in Shanxi, from Hebei and Shandong, and from as far away as Lhasa.

Until state intervention categorized the town as part of the core zone of a world heritage site, there was little demand for leasehold agricultural land in the valley. Under Chinese law, peasants cannot sell their land because they do not technically own it. Partly as a result of this, the compensation rates local officials offered to the first group of residents to be displaced in 2008 (between 400 and 1,200 yuan per meter, depending on different informants) probably reflected the market value of homes and farmland *if* world heritage plans were not taken into account. But once UNESCO granted world heritage status and the master plan was put into effect, compensation demands, as I will show, began to rise as well. The net result has not been a collective lament for a community lost but a fracturing of existing community ties. Those who have already been displaced believe they have been cheated, while those in line to be displaced are slated to receive vastly higher compensation rates. Meanwhile, some local residents argue that business owners who are outsiders (*waidi ren*) should not receive any compensation, and those who are not to be displaced in the near future welcome the erasure of their competitors and the monastic communities thrive.

At the macro level, the privatization of public housing and commercial space in China has been far more successful than in other socialist countries, particularly in the former Soviet Union. The Chinese process has not led to widespread homelessness, for example. Yet this process has invariably benefitted some state employees in cities and urban areas with strong economies, frozen younger employees in these areas out of housing markets, harmed many former and current state employees in depressed urban regions, and largely bypassed rural residents. But prosperity for some has also brought another consequence, the possibility of displacement.

A growing body of research both in China and abroad has examined the causes and consequences of the demolition of housing and the displacement of local residents in the name of development. Reform policies have enabled and facilitated particular classes of citizens to accumulate wealth and power, or what David Harvey has referred to as "accumulation through dispossession" through the poaching of state assets and the cultivation of personal and professional relationships (Zhang 2004:252). The Party-directed decentralization of managerial decision making that began in the 1980s has led central government ministries to cut direct funding to both provincial and local government affiliates and state enterprises. At the same time, state and Party officials increasingly have been evaluated not by their ideological correctness but by their development records, measured by economic growth. Faced with a need to generate much of their own budgets and demonstrate economic success, lower-level government officials have turned to the one asset they control: real estate. Selling use-rights for land under their jurisdiction to real estate companies generates revenue, at least in the short term. These real estate companies, often either state or quasi-state entities, then sell these use-rights to private developers (Fang and Zhang 2003:155–158). A 2001 State Council decree that authorized local authorities to appropriate land and carry out demolition for economic development programs has facilitated these policies (*Xinhua* 2011).

One result of the devolution of government funding has been the systematic displacement of residents from areas targeted for redevelopment. While in theory displaced people have a right to adequate compensation, local authorities usually set payment terms, often far below the actual value. More troublingly, numerous cases have been reported in the Chinese media of people who have refused to move and subsequently been threatened, beaten, and in some cases killed by thugs hired by real estate development companies. In addition, there have been several widely reported public suicides in protest of land seizures.

As public anger increased, national officials responded by publishing a draft housing compensation law in January 2010. Public law 590, which took effect on January 21, 2011, mandates that developers and local authorities pay displaced residents the actual market value of their homes, land, and businesses as well as moving related costs. The law bans forced removal and other coercive measures and places disputes in the civil court system. At the national level, the Legislative Affairs Office of the State

Council, the Ministry of Housing and Urban-Rural Development, and the Ministry of Land and Resources are tasked with jointly implementing and enforcing these new regulations (*Xinhua* 2011).

In June 2011, the Ministry of Land and Resources released regulations on determining compensation. Whereas in the past local authorities and real estate companies could arbitrarily set rates, the new rules allow residents to choose an independent appraisal company, and compensation rates must reflect actual market value (*China Daily* 2011). The decree specifies the purposes for which private holdings can be seized (transportation, education, diplomatic, energy, and defense-related projects) and also more important, those for which they cannot (commercial development) (GOC 2011).

However, significant questions remain. Under the new law, all affected owners must agree on an appraisal company, but only a simple majority has to agree to sell for a project to move forward. Moreover, the law does not address the issue of rural land seizures, where local government abuses are much more widespread (*The Economist* 2011). In addition, compensation claims are complicated by what many analysts argue is an unsustainable real estate market, as local authorities value land holdings at vastly inflated prices as collateral for loans used to fund large infrastructure projects intended to demonstrate economic growth. According to official statistics, state land sales revenue was $447 billion in 2010, more than 100 percent higher than in 2009. Without an alternative funding source, local authorities will continue to rely on land seizures and paper claims of artificially high land values as collateral on these loans. And, because most officials are evaluated on their economic performance in the short term, they have little incentive to care about the consequences of these loans or the long-term impact of current development projects because they have no intention of being around to grapple with the long-term consequences. Their goal typically is to be transferred up in the bureaucratic chain, meaning they will no longer be responsible.

This governance finance issue has directly impacted cultural resource management (CRM) policies in China. While central authorities in the Ministry of Culture and the State Administration for Cultural Heritage promote tourism at heritage sites as part of a moral and political campaign aimed at shaping personal behavior, local authorities tend to view heritage as an economic resource that can generate revenue for other development projects. Consequently, the Ministry of Culture issued China's first national guidelines for cultural heritage management, "Acts of World Heritage Site Protection and Management," in November 2006. This details how sites should be managed and maintained. Enforcement, however, remains a key problem primarily because the central government provides almost no direct funding for heritage projects.

All of these national issues (land seizures, housing and business demolition, disputes over compensation rates, and a (local) state claim of acting in the name of development) are present in the microcosm at Wutai Shan.

CREATIVE DESTRUCTION

The removal of Taihuai residents began in late 2007 and early 2008, shortly before the Ministry of Culture formally nominated Wutai Shan for World Heritage status as a national park centered on a core zone of Taihuai (GOC 2008b:35). During this first stage of displacement, houses and shops below Ta Yuan, Wofo, and Guangren temples were demolished and farmland north of town confiscated to build parkland, but not before residents sent a delegation to Beijing to present a petition to officials at the Ministry of Culture. The practice of petitioning national authorities has a long tradition in China and has been revived in the reform era. It is a practice that illustrates a central contradiction in state-society relations. While many citizens experience either state-sponsored or state-supported oppression in their everyday lives, many, particularly workers and peasants, distinguish between abuse and corruption at the experiential level of everyday life and the State and Party itself. Following this logic, some people believe that making their particular case known to national authorities will result in a policy change (Lee 2007). In other words, the State and Party are sometimes not held responsible for personal problems with representatives of both the State and Party because people believe that the former does not know what local authorities do in the name of the Party and national development.

The petition by Taihuai residents began by noting that people lived in the area before Buddhism arrived. It then describes how local residents have served Buddhist pilgrims for hundreds of years and also built many of the local temples. Finally, this letter argues that local residents had been on the right side of history during the Cultural Revolution because they had saved the temples of Wutai Shan from destruction, thereby enabling these to become world heritage:

> During the Cultural Revolution, when external rebel forces came to Wutai mountain to smash, beat and loot, the Red Guards carried three huge barrels of petrol to set fire to the temples, and it was the masses of Wutai mountain who risked their lives to battle the Red Guards, driving them out and therefore allowing Wutai mountain to escape the disaster of fire, enabling it to have the valuable resources it needs to apply for World Heritage today. (Anonymous 2008)

Therefore, residents assert their rights to remain at Taihuai based on longevity, service to Buddhism, and as defenders of this heritage site against revolutionary extremists. Yet they argue that they stand to gain no benefits from a world heritage designation. Being forced to move to the new satellite community of Jingangku would be "ungrateful and devoid of reason and emotion" as well as contrary to the "scientific development" promoted by the central government. The petition closes by using the reformist language of the Party itself to pose a challenge to heritage proponents:

> The ultimate goal for applying for World Heritage site is to accelerate social development, and to improve the living standards of people. Does the application for World Heritage status mean turning the site into a depopulated wasteland? Do successful World Heritage applications all over the world depend on damaging the interests of local residents? (Anonymous 2008)

The language of this petition illustrates a key point: residents are not overly concerned about authenticity and preservation. Instead, the authors focus on their own place in this community as both the builders and defenders of religious sites, remind readers that the Party's development goal is supposed to be to raise living standards, and suggest that world heritage actually hurts the interests of common people and thus social development. Rather than eradicating local communities, world heritage should be a development tool that improves local living standards.

Figure 4.1 A birds-eye view of Taihuai village from the Dailuo Terrace, 1992.

Figure 4.2 Taihuai 2008.

Nevertheless, where homes, shops, and fields once were is now a park space under construction, planted with trees and crisscrossed by stone paths. Figure 4.1 provides an overview of Taihuai, taken in 1992, while Figure 4.2 shows the same view in 2008. Using the White Pagoda of Tayuan temple as a visual marker illustrates the extent of demolition; almost nothing remains other than temple buildings. Marking this space as a heritage park is, incongruously, perhaps one of the cleanest and most up-to-date public restrooms in all of China. It has a pristine lobby with a flat screen television and toilet facilities that look as if they were lifted from Beijing's new international air terminal or one of the city's five-star hotels. Staff members keep the toilets spotless at all times, in part by preventing local residents from using them.

The park itself remains a work in progress (Figure 4.3). Lacking an irrigation system, it is usually dry and dusty in the summer months when most tourists visit. And, because there are few places to sit and planted trees have not yet matured, it is also largely empty during the daytime.

One afternoon, I encountered a park employee weeding grass by hand. He was not local but from a village near Taiyuan, the provincial capital, and only had the job because his boss had sent him to Taihuai. I asked him if he knew what had happened to the people who had once

Figure 4.3 Park construction in former residential area of Taihuai village, 2008.

lived there, and he shrugged. "*Na qian dou zou la*," he replied. "They took the money and left." But where did they go, I asked? "Away," he said vaguely. "The government paid them a lot of money. Now they don't have to work."

A local man who had stopped and listened interrupted.

> He doesn't know what he's talking about, he's not from here. Nobody went away! Where would they go? The young people, yes, they all have to go away these days to find work. But local people are still here. They're living here, out near Jinggangku, they are around. And nobody got paid a lot of money! Who does he think he is, talking about something he knows nothing about?

Below Dailuo Terrace, a handful of elderly residents sell religious objects such as prayer beads and wooden Buddha statues, along with dried fruits. They set out their wares on rocks alongside a horse trail that winds its way to the top. This is one of the few places in the area where people without licenses can still vend (Figure 4.4). It is also the worst area to try to sell souvenirs because almost all tourists either ride a cable car to the top of the ridge or walk up a 1,008 step stone staircase. Licensed

Figure 4.4 Some villagers who lost their land and homes sell souvenirs along tourist paths around local temples.

vendors, who typically number a hundred or more during the summer months, are restricted to an official market area at the base of the ridge, beside the town bus park and the cable car ticket office. But a permit to sell in this area costs 5,000 yuan per year, a sum many local people cannot afford. The net result is that not only are residents displaced but that the world heritage process transforms them into lawbreakers.

These vendors have little if anything to say about world heritage that is positive. One woman, sixty-one, laughed sarcastically when I asked her about world heritage. "World heritage doesn't help people, it's about making money. None of this is for us, life hasn't really changed for the common folk (*laobaixing*). Does anyone care about us these days?"

Born in 1951, she had come of age during the Cultural Revolution and spent her life as a peasant in Taihuai, during an era when peasants and workers were constantly evoked as models by the Communist Party. This is no longer the case. "Peasants don't contribute much to the country, do they?" she said to me. "That's the situation now."

> Look down there. Everything is destroyed. It's all been taken away, stolen. And over there (gesturing to her right) that side is going to be knocked down soon! There aren't many units (families) left. This area will all be

> torn down. That is it; later on there won't be people so there won't be anything interesting (*bu renao*). What's better? [Laughs]. The environment (*kongqi*) is much better nowadays, but life is worse. . . .

An elderly man chimed in:

> It's been going on four years since it was all knocked down. Now there are monks everywhere, but they should also have to go, too, right? The monks are rich! Where I used to live it has all become green. So what? It was green before! Fields are green! The country only cares about one thing, and it isn't to solve social problems. Even if people have enough food to fill their stomachs this doesn't solve the big problem. Nowadays China has no job allocation system (*fenpei*). Even if people graduate [from secondary school] they have to find their own work. There are too many students, too many graduates. All the work is with private companies (*siran danwei*) nowadays. The state work units don't have enough jobs for people.

Licensed vendors are not necessarily better off. Most sell the same type of objects, such as prayer beads, Buddhist statues, and umbrellas. None of these items are locally produced, and most vendors cannot afford to buy in bulk so they do not receive a wholesale price. For example, one woman who sells umbrellas at the official tourist market said she paid six yuan per item but could only sell these for eight yuan because of competition. On most days, she sold fewer than fifteen umbrellas. If she averaged fifteen sales per day and worked every day of the tourist season (April–October), her gross profit would be approximately 6,300 yuan for a year (900 yuan per month for 7 months). But the annual license fee to sell in the market costs 5,000 yuan. This would leave her with a net income of 1,300 yuan, or approximately $200. Service vendors did not do much better. For example, two middle-aged men have made a living for the past twenty years selling gimmick photographs in front of Xiankong temple. For a fee, they create photographs of tourists in clouds, as Buddha-like images emerging from the temple gates, or as miniatures standing in the palm of a friend. After their homes were demolished in 2008, these men rented rooms in town while their families moved to a village, one hour away by public bus, where they had relatives. Business is worse every year, they complained. Everyone has a digital camera and a cell phone and thinks they can be expert photographers, the one man said. When I mentioned that I had first visited the area in 1992, he asked if I had bought a photo from them. "We had already opened the door then" he said, referencing the beginning of the reform movement. "People like us were models for daring to take a chance on our own."

"You know," he added, "there were a lot more foreigners back then before Chinese could travel. There weren't so many visitors, but we made a better living. Chinese people don't want these things anymore."

A man working on a crew that was demolishing a brick wall near a recently built Buddhist Studies Institute shrugged when asked about displacement.

> This village is gone. It is a rule, a national rule. It has to do with world heritage. What's world heritage? You know, like a famous place (*mingshen*). Like a good scenic spot (*jingshan*), or a forest. The people who are gone got paid. Some of them have guesthouses or other businesses, but a lot are just gone. The government assigned families to new places. The government gave them money then sent them to Jingangku. How much did they get? Not enough.

THE ART OF MAKING DO

Three years after the revised Master Plan began to be implemented, much of the built space of Taihuai has disappeared (Figures 4.5 and 4.6). A young man who grew up in Taihuai and is now a tour guide explained that all of the land to the north of the town had once been farmland. It is now replanted with young evergreen trees. "We live in a park!" he said. He also repeated what several residents had said, that the remaining businesses in Taihuai would be removed soon, "maybe after the tourist season, maybe next year" [2012]. A woman who ran a restaurant with her husband along the town's main road suggested this was as much a national issue as a local one. "The national rule (*guojia guiding*) states that the heritage site must be cleared, so there is nothing we can do. This area along the main road was to have been cleared last year but nothing happened because there is no money to pay us." Another shopkeeper drew a distinction between complete demolition of the town, an abbreviated plan that did not displace all residents, and intervention by authorities at a higher level of government that would stop this demolition process:

> It is a money issue, you know? Who should be paid, how much, and by whom? If there is no money, then there won't be any more demolition. *Chai dao* [complete demolition], *chaibu dao* [planned demolition that does not reach this place], or *chaibuliao* [planned demolition blocked by new regulations or decisions], nobody is sure. The government doesn't have the money now, that's the problem.

Despite this uncertainty about funding and previous delays, many residents are resigned to losing their businesses and being moved. "It will be

Figure 4.5 Demolition of homes in Taihuai, 2008.

Figure 4.6 One of the few remaining commercial areas of Taihuai, 2011. This neighborhood is scheduled to be demolished by spring 2013.

grass" a restaurant owner said, talking about her building. "Like down there," she said, pointing toward the weedy park area that was once the other part of the town. "It will be a grass park." In the town bookstore, the manager laughed when asked what she would do after they were removed. "Who knows? We are supposed to go to Jingangku, but who will travel so far to buy a book?" A young man who came from a nearby village and ran his own restaurant speculated about moving. "We have to go, that's for sure," he said. "But maybe I will just take the money and do something else. No one knows what will happen at Jingangku or even where we can make businesses."

This tone of resignation is widely evident. The majority of residents not yet displaced accept the fact that the state, in the name of heritage as development, will do what it claims is best for the country. Yet any casual visitor to Taihuai cannot help but notice that preservation does not appear to be the main order of business. Indeed, while some temple restoration projects are being conducted, what is most evident, beyond the crowds of Chinese tourists and the partly constructed green spaces, is an intensive building boom. In fact, at the same time that entire neighborhoods in and around Taihuai have been demolished to meet the criteria for a buffer zone around what the nomination report refers to as "super sites," many local shops, hostels, and hotels are being renovated and expanded; dormitories are being constructed at several monasteries; and entire new temples are being built. This leads to two questions. The first is economic: why would people invest in renovating and expanding homes and businesses that they believe will be demolished within the next year? The second is a managerial and bureaucratic question: how and why are monasteries and temples that have been listed as world heritage sites being not just restored but expanded? How is this apparent flouting of preservation guidelines possible to such a degree, particularly in a country that many observers believe is ruled by a one party authoritarian state? These two types of ongoing construction projects in the wake of the demolition of much of Taihuai illustrate the complexities and social and cultural specificities of heritage at Wutai Shan.

Investments in local homes and businesses are an example of a phenomenon known in Chinese as *qiangjian*, which translates as "snatching or stealing" (*qiang*) and "constructing" (*jian*). This term is used to describe a process in which people strategically invest in renovations when they know they will be displaced. By investing in a property that is certain to be demolished, owners increase their compensation rates by taking advantage of increasingly complex national displacement regulations. As already noted, in response to popular complaints about unfair compensation and the use of force by real estate developers to harass and remove residents blocking projects, the national government has instituted new compensation regulations. In seeking to measure fair market value, these regulations require developers to pay for all aspects of a built structure. This includes not just total size but also the quality of building materials, its location, and its use. This in turn suggests that residents subject to displacement should receive different compensation rates, as explained by an official with the district world heritage management office to a colleague:

> The compensation for the residents in Phase I was based on a complicated metrics: such as by size, location, function, and building materials. For instance, they differentiate residence, business use, and mixed use; and if the house is built with clay, brick, or cement. The money was from all administrative levels: the provincial government, city government, county government, and district government.

The most immediate result of this state attempt to objectively measure the value of built space has not been public acceptance of the process as either more transparent or fairer. Instead, this has spurred a new type of construction boom, focused on short-term renovations that will increase compensation rates, a profoundly different type of creative destruction than that imagined by most free market economists or Karl Marx. It is also a process that further contributes to a local atmosphere of distrust because what appears to be transparent is not a fair process of measuring value but a complex system that enables unequal outcomes.

In a neighborhood scheduled for demolition beside the Dailuo cable car, an old man squatted at the door of an unfinished three story house, eating lunch. The building was unfinished because the district government had halted construction for building code violations. "No one is supposed to have a building with three stories," he said. The old man was not alone; his street had five more unfinished buildings. Another man, a retired Party cadre, said the district government was trying to prevent *qiangjian*, so had decreed new height limits. In response to complaints, however, they had backtracked, revising the new regulations to allow renovations on existing buildings if owners removed third floors, rather than demanding complete demolition.

This local ordinance had not stopped the construction of several new buildings that clearly violated this building code. A woman in her early forties who sold souvenirs without a license laughed at the idea that compensation was either fair or transparent. She used to live on Taiping Road near the center of town, where her family owned a small guesthouse. In 2010, the district government had paid 2,800 yuan per meter for their property of 175 square meters, a total of 490,000 yuan. This was at least double, and depending on different respondents, as much as seven times the compensation rate paid to the first residents to be displaced in 2008. This did not mean this woman was satisfied. She said the government paid the same compensation to all residents, no matter the quality or use of their properties. "But the ones with *guanxi* (connections) were paid a lot more," she claimed. They also were given access to new jobs as service workers in the park zone or as bus drivers. She now was renting a small room in town that she shared with her husband and son and said she would move to the resettlement town near Jingangku. "But the government hasn't paid the developer," she complained. "So no one can move yet."

State investments in the Wutai Shan project are concentrated in two adjacent sites near the village of Jingangku, twenty-three kilometers south of Taihuai and a few kilometers inside the south gate of the new park. A National Park and World Heritage center is under construction nearby, consisting of a visitor center and museum, an exhibition hall, a shopping complex, and an international resort, while on the edge of the village a satellite housing community has been completed.

As of June 2012, the service complex had been finished, along with an enormous (but empty) parking lot, and resort construction had just been started. Meanwhile, the new housing at Jingkanku intended for displaced Taihuai residents remained mostly empty, although the complex had been completed in the spring of 2010. By counting the water tanks on roofs, I estimated that 10% of the homes were occupied in June 2011. On one visit, I spoke with a middle-aged peasant and his relatively young wife. She had worked in a shoe factory in southern China for two years before returning to the area. For no discernible reason, they were sitting on an empty sidewalk in a light rain, having lunch, she a chicken drumstick, he a dried fish with a bottle of beer. They said the houses cost 1,000 yuan a square meter and were "very modern." You had to be from Taishan (Taihuai) to qualify, the woman said. At one of the few occupied houses, an elderly man said he had paid 1,200 yuan a square meter for his home but wondered when he would have neighbors. Although not particularly well built (some walls already have cracks and some of the homes are missing roof tiles), this publicly financed housing is of relatively good quality and comparable to equivalent housing in cities such as Beijing (Figure 4.7). So why does a new complex designed to house 1,857 households and 6,500 people remain largely empty two years after being completed, especially in a country that faces an ongoing housing crisis?

"Those houses haven't been allocated yet," an elderly man said. "The authorities still have to determine who qualifies."

"They cost too much," a woman asserted. "When you multiple the price per square meter by the size, no one has that kind of money."

Figure 4.7 Jingangku new housing complex, 2011. Most of these homes remained empty as of summer 2012.

"The people who lost their land don't want to move so far away," said another woman. "How will they get back and forth to Taihuai?"

"It's a money problem," explained a man who drove an unlicensed cab, echoing the woman who had lost her guesthouse. "The government doesn't have the money to pay the builder, so he won't turn over the keys."

"It's a land problem," asserted another man. "The people who should live here are peasants. They lost their land, and these new places don't give owners land rights."

Contrary to what the official cited above suggests, the central government, as is the case with almost all heritage projects in China, provides no direct funding, while the Shanxi provincial government's assistance is limited to paying the interest on project loans. An official in the district government suggested that as of 2010 approximately 1 billion yuan ($153 million) had already been borrowed. The overall cost of the twenty-year project is estimated to be 5.3 billion yuan (approximately $800 million) by 2025. These loans are supposed to pay for land acquisition, structural improvements, new tourist facilities, and park staffing costs. They are also supposed to cover all compensation costs for displacement, including the costs associated with acquiring land near Jingangku and the construction of the new housing complex.

As noted earlier, a practical bureaucratic problem is overall responsibility. The district government is responsible for paying these loans, but the officials who arranged the loans in the first place will be gone from their positions when payment is due. This is because job performance at the district level in China is primarily evaluated on economic development criteria. If officials can demonstrate that they have achieved development, they will be promoted. A second problem is the potential corruption a project of this size creates. One informant suggested that people could receive larger compensation rates for their properties if they agreed to return a percentage to district officials. In addition, lucrative contracts have been disbursed for the demolition of homes and businesses in Taihuai, the construction of new housing in Jingangku and the park tourist center, and the purchase of a fleet of new buses for a local transportation system within the park boundaries.

But the largest factor may turn out to be compensation. As of the summer of 2011, residents slated to be resettled in the coming year believed the rate per square meter for homes and businesses would be as high as 9,000 yuan, at least seven times as much as paid to those first displaced. For people with a small guest house of one hundred square meters, this translates into a compensation package of approximately $140,000—a sum most would have found unimaginable a decade ago. Nevertheless, some are not satisfied.

"What can I do?" one shopkeeper asked. "That [government payments] still won't provide me an income. If they move me to the south gate, I will lose all of my business. But you do what the government wants, that's the way things work." This man said his shop and home were approximately 120 square meters which, if his estimates are correct, means he will receive almost one million yuan (approximately $160,000) in compensation. As this example illustrates, the total cost of continued displacement, especially if the new national compensation law is effective and local strategies of *qiangjian* succeed, are staggering.

MARKETING RELIGION

As noted in Chapter III, the Mount Wutai management plan prohibits new construction at listed temple sites within the core zone. The plan states that "only maintenance and conservation of cultural relics is allowed, while new construction, expansion and renovation are prohibited" (GOC 2008b:239). It also asserts that "architectural authenticity and integrity are not to be impaired in the name of religion" (241), "there shall be no reconstruction of disappeared heritage in principle"

(239), and finally, "new construction or expansion to the temples is strictly controlled" (294). Nevertheless, widespread temple construction projects are underway within the core zone. Not only are temples being renovated and repainted, guestrooms and dormitories have also been constructed to serve a growing demand by visitors. World heritage status, although intended to safeguard listed sites from tourism, has stimulated a revival of a local economy of religious practice. This includes everything from the sale of incense and amulets at temples and short-term residency in monasteries to the performance of private prayer services for affluent visitors and private consultations with monks. For example, one informant reported that a private prayer service at the Wuye Temple can cost as much as 30,000 Yuan (approximately $4,500). Thus, if heritage status has significantly harmed many local residents through displacement, it has opened up new forms of income for both monastic communities and prominent monks, as I will discuss in more detail in Chapter V.

In a technical sense, the management authorities of Wutai National Park remain in compliance with both the master plan and the management and conservation plan, and thus, by implication, with UNESCO guidelines. This is because of the unusual context of the park itself. Within the core zone, local residents and businesses have either been removed or are scheduled to be removed. However, what will remain will not be only protected heritage sites. UNESCO did not grant world heritage status to the entire park area, as local officials had wanted. Instead, eight temples (Xiantong, Pusa, Tayuan, Bishan, Shuxiang, Nanshan, Longquan, and Jinge) in the core zone along with Foguang Temple, located twenty kilometers outside the park boundaries, have been inscribed collectively on the world heritage list as "Mount Wutai." In addition to these world heritage sites, the core zone of Wutai National Park also contains approximately thirty more temples and monasteries, none of which are bound to the building restrictions associated with heritage preservation. It is these religious sites that are expanding rapidly, stimulated by a resurgence of interest in Buddhism among Chinese, a Party and State acceptance of strictly apolitical religious institutions, and the commercialization of all aspects of life within the People's Republic, including worship. This burst of expansion goes beyond income generation, however; it also includes completely new construction.

A recent UNESCO guide to world heritage sites includes one photograph in its description of Wutai Shan. Picturing an unnamed temple, the caption reads, "One of the many temples on Mount Wutai" (UNESCO 2010:802). Yet the temple depicted in this photograph is not one of the sites inscribed by UNESCO. Instead, it is the newest temple in the area, completed in 2011 (Figure 4.8). Located on a ridge below Dailuo terrace, Wenshu (Manjusri) Temple has a commanding view of Taihuai and the core heritage zone. A temple of the same name, built during the Song Dynasty (960–1279), stood on the same site more than one thousand years ago. After falling into disrepair, this original Wenshu temple was rebuilt at a new location during the reign of the Qing Emperor Kangxi (1736–1795). This Qing-era temple still exists, south of the center of Taihuai along the east bank of the Qingshui River. It is this Wenshu temple that is listed in guidebooks. The new Wenshu temple appears neither in guidebooks nor on any tourist maps. Instead, its location on the official tour map of Wutai Shan is a blank green space. According to a senior monk, construction was funded by the district administrative office (*zhangguan*) along with private donations. "This is on the exact spot that it used to be," he said. "It isn't new."

This view—that a new temple is not in fact new because it is a restoration of the past—illustrates the continued relevance of Chinese perceptions of the relationship between built space, originality, and authenticity, and how these differ from the ontologically centered values that organizations such as UNESCO promote. To call this new

Figure 4.8 The new Wenshu Temple, nearing completion after a four-year building project.

temple a copy of a former temple and therefore a fake makes no sense. Instead, this new construction has restored this sacred landscape to how it once was.

This view also illustrates the gap between preservationist perspectives on tourism and those of monastic community members in the area. For example, a few hundred meters behind the parking lot for the tourist reception center and luxury resort complex being built on former rice fields near the south gate of the park is a small temple. It sits alone, surrounded by a plastered wall of faded and peeling paint. Haihui Temple was built during the late Ming Dynasty, renovated in the late Qing Dynasty and early Republican era, but since 1913 has been untouched. It is a small, quiet temple complex, home to perhaps a dozen Buddhist nuns. Although open to visitors, it receives very few. Inside the walls, its courtyard contains several ancient cypress trees, a central hall dedicated to Manjusri, and a small secondary hall with a collection of vivid and graphic wall murals depicting the different forms of suffering awaiting people in hell. The residents of Haihui seemed nonplussed by the prospect of tourists; what bothers them was their lack of visitors, not the supposed problems visitors might bring.

"So many temples in Taishan [Taihuai] have been renovated!" one nun said. "The tourists and pilgrims have paid for that."

"And the government, too," said another.

They both looked forward to the opening of the enormous new tourism complex and resort being built literally in their backyard. "Then we will get money, too, and can fix this place up."

It makes no sense to assume these pious Buddhist nuns would be critics of tourism and opponents of change. Far from believing tourism and state-sanctioned development was a threat, they saw both as an opportunity to rebuild, restore, and increase the standing of their small community. Though on the surface Haihui temple looks as if it has been preserved for the past century (in the sense of not having been changed), this is not from choice but from neglect. Being an out-of-the-way temple in a valley filled with temples, its nun caretakers have not had access to funding to do what would be normal, to replenish and restore this site as an ongoing and organic worship space. Instead, it has become a living museum, seemingly frozen in time.

In summary, the decision to categorize the Wutai area as a national park and a world heritage site has been economically beneficial to some local monastic communities while others seek to get their share. First, the UNESCO endorsement of eight temples within the park proper as world heritage sites has had the effect of adding value to Wutai National Park in the domestic competition for tourists. World Heritage status justifies not just the hefty admission fee to the Park (168 yuan per person) but more importantly the entire Wutai Shan development project. The net effect has been high visitor totals, especially during the summer months. In addition, the state framing of the park boundaries has transformed the geographic space within the core zone into a new type of sacred space, the sacred space of the secular world heritage movement. And the values of this movement, in particular a foundational assumption that heritage space must be protected from the corrupting effects of market forces, have led to a process (the displacement of local businesses) that benefit monasteries and temples by erasing market competition for pilgrims and other visitors. This explains why so many temples and monasteries are building hostels: once the master plan is fully implemented in 2025, only religious institutions will be able to offer accommodation within the core zone. From a monastic perspective, separating sacred and commercial space does not protect them from the dangers of commerce but erases competition for pilgrims and tourists, thereby helping them increase their own revenues. There is, however, a problem for religious institutions. These are communities filled with monks, nuns, students, and visitors, all of whom need to engage in daily commerce, such as buying food, clothing, snacks, and the like. Many of the small businesses that will be displaced are in the business of religion, such as noodle stalls, tea shops, and clothing stores. It is not clear what will happen if this plan is fully implemented and all commercial businesses within the core zone are eliminated.

One clue to understanding what on the surface appears to be a maze of contradictions—a new satellite town largely empty of residents, local entrepreneurs investing in businesses that may soon be demolished, monasteries engaged in a frenzy of new construction—is the complicated bureaucratic structure that governs Wutai. In short, different parts of "The State" have different interests, not all of which necessarily overlap. Overall authority for Wutai National Park resides with the Ministry of Construction and the Construction Authority of Shanxi Province (GOC 2008a:301). However, forest management in the valley falls under the purview of the State Forestry Administration, formerly the Ministry of Forestry until 1998 when it was placed under the direct authority of the State Council, the highest governing body in the PRC. The preservation of temple sites is the responsibility of the State Administration of Cultural Heritage, which is supposed to cooperate with the Ministry of Culture. The State Administration for Religious Affairs regulates practice at temples and monasteries, and the State Ethnic Affairs Commission oversees Tibetans, Mongolians, and other ethnic minorities living within the park boundaries. Geological sites fall under the domain of the Ministry of Geology, while fossils are the responsibility of the Ministry of Land and Resources. Finally, the

National Tourism Administration is supposed to promote the park as a tourist destination. These vertical ties clash not only with each other but also with a different set of state actors emanating from the Shanxi provincial government down to Taihuai municipal authorities. For example, national heritage sites located outside the official boundaries of Wutai National Park fall under the domain of the Shanxi Provincial Cultural Heritage Bureau and provincial heritage sites outside the park are managed by county-level bureaus (GOC 2008b:7, 13). However, all sites, of whatever designation, located within the park boundaries fall under the authority of the Religion and Heritage Administration Bureau of the People's Government of Mount Wutai National Park, while each monastery has its own management committee (GOC 2008a:249). To make this bureaucratic maze even more complicated, twenty-nine different international, national, and provincial conventions, laws, and decrees impact the overall site. These range from the 1972 Convention on World Heritage and various State Council decrees on heritage protection to national laws regulating geological heritage (1995), forests (1998), fossils (2002), cultural relics (2003), religious practice (2004), and scenic areas (2006).

The anonymous authors of the petition local residents wrote to national authorities in Beijing assume that heritage projects have as their main goal social development. Yet it is clear that the process of socially constructing history and culture is a process rooted in the exercise of power, enabling those who hold it to clean up the past. This is an exercise in "authenticity-as-impression-management" (Gable and Handler 1998:575). An example is the "old towns" and restored historic districts increasingly found in China. Although many of these sites can point to great success in historical preservation, how the past is preserved and what aspects are highlighted are crucial issues. In other words, "the past" is not preserved but rather some aspects of the past, while other stories are, if not erased, then not mentioned. This process is the form cultural heritage takes, whether in China, the United States, or elsewhere. Balancing competing interests at heritage sites is therefore not only a bureaucratic issue nor simply a UNESCO issue; it is rooted in the fundamental logic of "cultural heritage." Sites, no matter if they are cultural, or natural, or some combination of these, always have contested histories.

Heritage unfolds in surprising and at times unpredictable ways in China. Sites and objects that were either neglected or actively destroyed in the past, and people who were at best tolerated but usually treated as suspected traitors to the Revolution, have been transformed into "heritage." Religious practice may still be called feudal superstition but it is also presented as part of China's heritage and evidence of a long and unified Chinese history. In this narrative, Wutai Shan is a symbol of Chinese culture because, according to signboards scattered about Taihuai, it is "one of the world's five most important Buddhist places." This controlled cultivation of religious performance at Wutaishan is built, ironically, on the ruins of post-1949 socialist development and modernization. But contrary to project intentions, this revival has not taken on a performative guise. Instead, rather than a dioramic rendition of Buddhism-as-culture, what is produced and consumed at the temples and monasteries of Wutai is Buddhism-as-practice.

Chapter V

Chao Xiang, Bai Fo, & Lü You

Pilgrimage, Worship, and Tourism

In the past two decades, the field of tourism studies has expanded far beyond a critique of the presumed destruction of authentic culture at the hands of an all-pervasive mass tourism, a common theme in earlier work (cf. MacCannell 1976; Greenwood 1977). This earlier research implicitly linked the overpopulation concerns of conservationists with a suspicion of mass consumerism and cultural commodification that has its roots in the work of theorists such as Walter Benjamin. While this commodification approach remains popular among globalization critics who bemoan a supposedly "McDonaldization" of the world, tourism researchers in a variety of fields and disciplines increasingly are cognizant of the fluidity of cultural practices and norms; the role of factors such as gender, age, socioeconomic class, and ethnicity in tourist–local encounters; and the decentering of Europe and North America in the discussion of the source of tourist flows (Winter 2007). Yet these changes also bring new research challenges, not least of which are the practical and theoretical limits to a wholesale embrace of an unreflective social constructivism that questions the value of any empirical claims.

This is because, in seeking to understand how the world heritage process unfolds at a place such as Wutai Shan, certain questions can best be answered with empirical evidence. For example, what types of people visit this world heritage site and why? To what extent can visitors be classified as pilgrims, religious tourists, cultural tourists, nature lovers, or seekers of new and different experiences? What role does the state, which remains officially atheistic, play in visitor motivations? Do these questions even matter anymore, or would it be more accurate to assert that in a postmodern world, pigeonholing intentions is an exercise in

Faith in Heritage: Displacement, Development, and Religious Tourism in Contemporary China by Robert J. Shepherd, 121–147

futility and no essential differences can be discerned between a pilgrim and a tourist? The latter question has been debated among scholars in and between the related fields of tourism studies, the anthropology of tourism, and the anthropology of religion.

An increasing number of scholars in all three fields have embraced what is typically referred to in the literature as a postmodern perspective on tourist motivations. In its rigid form, this approach directly challenges the very basis of field research by asserting that all truths are contingent. This is a view rooted in the work of French scholars such as Michel Foucault, Jean Baudrillard, and Jean-François Lyotard. In his *Archeology of Knowledge* (1969), Foucault emphasized the production of meaning within specific places and periods, rather than a search for a deeper or transcendental truth or set of truths. According to Baudrillard in his *For a Critique of the Political Economy of the Sign* (1981), what we observe around us is merely a collection of signs, so no particular interpretation of these signs is any more valid than another, while Lyotard, writing in *The Postmodern Condition* (1979), asserted that no truths in the form of metanarratives exist. All three French theorists owe a crucial debt to Friedrich Nietzsche, a vehement critic of both empiricism and positivism. This ideological stance is not only skeptical of empiricism but is often anti-empirical and should give one pause to consider what it implies for ethnographic research on tourist motivations.

From a postmodern perspective, people travel for a multitude of reasons, and even at a religious site, ostensibly faith-driven visitors engage in a range of behaviors. They may pray, travel along a predetermined route, visit a set number of shrine-like destinations, and yet also eat well, shop for souvenirs, and, broadly speaking, "have fun," thereby collapsing any distinctions among secular and religious, serious and playful, contemplation and entertainment. Evoking postmodernism as a catch-all label to explain behavior has become quite common in tourism studies, albeit too often in a manner that is neither well conceptualized nor contextualized. For example, Nuryanti (1996) argues that postmodern tourism is defined by its emphasis on "individual journeys of self-discovery" (250). Similarly, Collins-Kreiner and Kliot (2000) assert that the behavioral differences between pilgrims and tourists have decreased to the point where maintaining divisions is of little value. In her more recent work, Collins-Kreiner (2010) has declared that "no place is intrinsically sacred" (444), "each person may interpret his or her own experience differently" (448), and that consequently, "issues of 'right' and 'wrong' seem less important in the post-modern world, and may not even exist" (450). This is a view endorsed by Maoz and Beckerman (2010), who reject any distinctions between either pilgrims and tourists or religious tourists and what they label "New Age ones" (436). Writing specific about tourism in China,

Oakes and Sutton (2010) see a convergence of tourist and pilgrim intentions, asserting that pilgrims act as tourists while tourists may engage in religious practices. The most extreme view holds that a pilgrimage can be any sort of journey that is "redolent with [personal] meaning" (Digance 2006:36). Even when a visitor has no personal experience, cultural connection, or belief linking her to a sacred site, she can nevertheless share a sacred experience because, apparently, "the heartfelt desire to enter a special time and place is no more than something that is part of humankind's existence" (45). The claim to a shared universal experience echoes the language of other transnational discourses such as human rights. In both cases, the existence of a category of human experience is taken as evidence of a experiential sameness, despite empirical differences. Thus, while cosmological belief is, like social reproduction rituals such as marriage, a universal human category, the ways in which this is put into practice are culturally particular. In other words, just because humans share a desire to experience an extraordinary event does not mean they do so in universally understandable ways.

The anthropological literature on tourism and pilgrimage also has tended to conflate these terms, beginning with Victor and Edith Turner's influential work on pilgrimage (1978). They characterized the pilgrimage process as an extraordinary life event that removes participants from their everyday routines. "Betwixt and between" stable social spaces and adrift in liminality, pilgrim-travelers construct new forms of *communitas* as they grapple with being out of place, after which they return home, renewed (see also Graburn 1977). In the decades since the Turners' book appeared, many anthropologists have argued that the pilgrimage process is not limited to religious intentions. Instead, whether as a collective experience or as a search for self-renewal, a wide variety of travel actions that are not formally religious can nevertheless serve a sacred-like purpose (Badone and Roseman 2004:2). Thus, a pilgrimage can be to most any popular destination, whether a memorial site, natural site, amusement park, or religious space: what is "sacred" is profoundly individual and hence resists categorization (Reader and Walter 1993).

In their recent article on an international Buddhist festival at Wutai Shan arranged by provincial authorities to publicize the area's world heritage status, Chris Ryan and Gu Huimin (2009) offer a highly descriptive overview of this festival event. Aptly noting that researchers are part of what they observe, they hesitate to offer any interpretative findings, stating that any such interpretation is "opaque" and limited (11). Their implication is that one cannot categorize visitor intentions nor rank these in terms of substance or engagement.

Such an approach erases all differences between visitor intentions. In doing so, it does not just flatten out culturally specific reasons for travel but also may ignore that people do, in fact, visit religiously marked sites in arguably any society for different reasons, some of which are clearly religious, in the sense of being motivated by supernatural goals, desires, or intentions (Eade and Sallnow 1991). Moreover, because a tourism-as-pilgrimage perspective assumes the *extra*ordinary foundations of pilgrimage, it neglects the extent to which such journeys may not be a quest for liminality but instead an aspect of everyday life (Coleman and Eade 2004). One response to this critique is to offer a mediating category between pilgrim and tourist, namely religious tourist (Badone and Roseman 2004:10), a perspective shared by Cohen (1992a).

This approach is often found in Chinese tourism literature. Zhang et al. (2007) describe religious tourism as "a special tourist activity orientated by religious culture with the help of a specific eco-cultural environment" (101). They also assert that most Han Chinese do not believe in religion and therefore visit historic pilgrimage sites such as Wutai Shan for cultural and historical reasons. They are thus "cultural pilgrims" (105). This is a common state claim as well. For example, in a recent introductory guide to ethnicity and religion in China, the author estimated that approximately 100 million citizens (out of a population of 1.3 billion) are religious believers in China, only 10 million of whom are Han Chinese (Zhang 2010:148).

Religious destinations, particularly Buddhist sites, such as Wutai Shan that attract an ethnic cross-section of visitors, are described by tourism authorities as "religious-cultural tourism" (*zongjiao wenhua luyou*) destinations, while state officials in organizations such as the Religious Affairs Commission focus on managing, not banning, Buddhist practices (by pilgrims, monks, and tourists) (Kang, 2009). This approach is similar to central government policies that are designed to manage and not erase Tibetan quotidian cultural practices in the Tibetan Autonomous Region and other areas in China.

The current emphasis on a postmodern erasure of all differences between pilgrims and tourists raises several questions, beginning with its anthropologically thin basis. First of all, to characterize a pilgrimage site as any place a group of people travels to not only negates any differences between a destination valued for its cosmological significance and one valued for other reasons, it also negates the very notion of sacred space (Timothy and Olsen 2006). A necessary questioning of categories does not mean that differences do not in fact exist among visitors to religious sites (Eade and Sallnow 1991). Yet in recognizing different intentions, it does not follow that people who visit a pilgrimage site have unique *individual* reasons for doing so. Such a neoliberal perspective removes actually existing beings from their culturally embedded frames of reference and reimagines them to be autonomous actors making discreet personal choices as portrayed in the neoclassical economics tradition. From this perspective, *all* interpretations must logically be valid.

This in turn points to a theoretical contradiction. If no transcendental truths exist and all claims to universals are to be rejected as metafictions, why should a claim that all interpretations everywhere are merely performative acts of sign-reading also not be rejected as a fictitious meta-claim? Moreover, if all interpretations, being subjective, are in the end merely interpretations, why privilege a particular interpretation, including that of a researcher? Why not publish the musings of a *Lonely Planet* backpacker and call this research?

In regards to religious destinations, the (productive) deconstruction of universally suspect categories such as tourist and traveler in the name of a universal claim of *no* categories ignores the contextual realities of actually existing pilgrimage sites. As Cohen (1992b) has noted, proclaiming tourism to be a form of pilgrimage is questionable not because differences among visitor motivations do not exist but because the analysis this view draws from (Turner and Turner 1978) was based on Christian pilgrimage sites and thus may not be applicable in other cultural settings. Given that destinations historically identified as pilgrimage sites are embedded in a culturally thick grammar that explains the reasons for such a status, it logically follows that cultural outsiders will simply not have the requisite knowledge, let alone the language skills, to understand a site or set of practices. This illustrates an epistemological (social) fact: some interpretations are more useful because these are comparative and analytical rather than descriptive and self-referential (Errington and Gewertz 2009:103). In other words, some observers have more information, experience, or a combination of these about a given event than do other observers, which is reflected in how they interpret an event. Thus, recognizing that particular sacred destinations attract visitors who may not believe does not negate the sacred quality of those who do. For a place to be sacred, whether in a religious sense (such as Varanasi in India or Lourdes in France) or a secular sense (such as Graceland in Memphis or the baseball Hall of Fame in Cooperstown, New York), one must understand and experience this sacredness (Bremer 2006). Finally, as Winter (2007) has argued, many studies of postmodern tourists continue to assume that tourists are implicitly Western, an assumption that is factually invalid in China, where the overwhelming majority of tourists are either domestic Chinese or regional arrivals.

According to official statistics, the vast majority of visitors to Wutai Shan in 2007, a year before it was formally nominated as a World Heritage site and two years before it achieved World Heritage status, were domestic tourists. In fact, pilgrims accounted for less than 10% of all visitors. Even in the most popular month (August), only 59,400 of a total of 575,000 arrivals were classified as religious pilgrims (GOC 2008b:233). In conversations with a local official in Taihuai in 2010, I was told that only 1 in 8 visitors came for religious reasons. The rest were tourists, he explained.

This statistical claim supports the state view that few Han Chinese practice religion. From the state perspective, tourists visit Wutai Shan because it is a historical and cultural destination that demonstrates China's long history. By doing so, they help alleviate poverty with their vacation spending and increase local citizen quality (*suzhi*). From the perspective of UNESCO and related institutions such as ICOMOS, Wutai Shan is a world heritage site that to some degree should be protected from the economic successes of the Chinese reform program that has increased domestic tourism. The tension between the economic and social development goals of the central Chinese state and the material preservationist goal of UNESCO is quite common at heritage sites in China. In reality, relatively few people visit Wutai Shan strictly as tourists. Instead, most people who visit are Chinese citizens who intend to *baifo* (literally "to worship Buddha") in some manner. These visitors include Han, Mongolian, and Tibetan monks and pilgrims; elderly women on a contemporary form of pilgrimage; others, mainly women, on short visits to study at monasteries or at a recently opened Buddhist studies institute; state employees on government-funded group junkets; extended families; and the occasional small group of men, often relatively young, seeking to gain a bit of good fortune. Missing are foreigners, particularly Europeans and North Americans, who do not visit in any significant number.

However, it would be wrong to assume that local officials make up statistical data or deliberately seek to deceive. This is instead an example of how visitor categories are socially and therefore *culturally* constructed. Quite simply, there is no reliable way for either national park or local government officials to know precisely who visits Wutai Shan for what reasons through statistical data because there are no entry forms to complete when entering the park. People line up, buy tickets, and walk through a turnstile, much as if they were entering a sport stadium. Ethnicity, nationality, gender, and purpose of visit are not asked. Only in extraordinary circumstances can *waidi* (nonlocal) people avoid paying the hefty admission fee. County residents do not have to pay, nor do monks and nuns affiliated with local religious institutions. The only other outsiders who are exempt from admission fees are monks and nuns who demonstrate they are on a pilgrimage to Wutai Shan, by, for example, appearing at one of the entry gates on foot, shaving their heads, and wearing robes. As for how authorities classify who is a tourist and who is a religious visitor, there appears to be no clear criteria. One official at the north entrance to the park zone said they calculated these numbers by tabulating hotel registration records. However, local registration forms do not require people to state the purpose of their visit. Another official said that they relied on head counts at temple sites. This also is puzzling, because all visitors, no matter their purpose in visiting, can be found at famous temples, precisely because religious sites are the main attraction. The most likely basis of these statistics is ethnicity: the roughly 10% of arrivals who are classified as "religious tourists" are, I suspect, Mongolians and Tibetans. Conflating the historical record of Wutai Shan (its importance as a pilgrimage site for Mongolians and Tibetans after the Manchurian conquest of China in the seventeenth century) with the political discourse of post-1949 socialism (minority peoples have superstitions such as religion, Han Chinese do not), local authorities assume that Mongolians and Tibetans are motivated by religion, while Han Chinese are not.

Who Visits Wutai Shan?

The lack of reliable statistical data for determining visitor origins and intentions does not mean that a snapshot portrayal of these issues cannot be offered. A sense of who visits Wutai Shan and why is obtainable through the use of both qualitative and quantitative data. Therefore, the claimed "facts" that supposedly emerge from a rigid statistical approach should not be assumed to contest the "impressions" associated with a qualitative analysis. Surveying, interviewing, and counting complement rather than clash with observing, discussing, and participating. Thus, I am skeptical of divisions between hard and soft, objective and subjective, or scientific and humanistic; when you can count, by all means count. But when you cannot, or when doing so does not provide a full rendering of the social complexities of a place (which it never does), then venture beyond surveys to observe and converse (Bruner 2010). The outcome will not be a set of objectively rigid truths but a collection of insights and hints into how people engage in the experiential stuff of life.

To better understand the reasons why people visit Wutai Shan, I gathered such data with a cohort of researchers during the summers of 2010 and 2011. In July 2010, a formal survey was conducted primarily by Chinese graduate students majoring in tourism management at a national university in Beijing. Tourists were surveyed outside one of the most popular temples (Wuye), at Taihuai Bus Station, and at several local hotels. A total of 228 responses were collected, of which 175 (76.8%) were complete. Of these respondents, 102 (58%) were male and 73 (42%) were female. Geographically, respondents came from 14 provinces, although the largest number (67) were residents of Shanxi province, in which Wutai Shan is located, and approximately 25%

were from Beijing. In July 2011, I returned to Taihuai and conducted qualitative interviews with tourists. A total of 215 respondents were interviewed at four temples: Xietong, Tayuan, Pusa (all world heritage sites), and Dailuo terrace. Of this total, 123 interviewees were women and 92 were men. Again, the majority were from Shanxi (83) and Beijing (56). In both the 2010 survey and 2011 interviews, respondents were asked where they were from, how long they planned to stay at Wutai Shan, and why they had decided to visit.

Taken collectively, this data demonstrates that a majority of tourists to Wutai Shan come either from Shanxi or from the northern region of China (Inner Mongolia, Hebei, Henan provinces and Beijing, Tianjin municipalities). The 2010 survey found that visitors were relatively well educated and affluent. One-third of respondents had attended a four-year college, one-quarter a three-year college, and 11.6% held graduate degrees, while approximately 75% had a yearly family income of more than 20,000 yuan ($3,000), of which 23.3% earned more than 50,000 yuan ($8,000) annually.

Most significant, a majority of survey respondents in 2010 (116 of 175, 66%) indicated that religion was their primary reason for visiting Wutai Shan, followed by vacation (17%) and business (9%). To test these findings, I provided respondents in 2011 with four reasons for visiting Wutai Shan and asked them to choose their primary purpose. These were worshipping (*baifo*), pilgrimage (*chaoxiang*), tourism (*lü you*), or "field trips" (*kaocha*; see below). The results mirrored our 2010 findings, as illustrated below:

Table 5.1 Primary purpose for visiting Wutai Shan

Purpose	Percentage of total	Number of women	Number of men
Baifo	65.1	81	59
Luyou	8.9	9	10
Chaoxiang	12.1	23	3
Kaocha	13.9	10	20

Table 5.2 Average length of stay for men and women

Length of stay	Percentage of total	Number of women	Number of men
3–5 days	31.2	57	10
1–2 days	58.1	44	81
5 or more days	10.7	22	1

R = 215

When queried about their length of stay, a majority of these 2011 respondents (125) said they intended to visit for two days or less. This illustrates an unintended consequence of improved access to Wutai Shan. A new national highway that will by the summer of 2012 provide direct access to the park with major urban areas has reduced travel time between Beijing and Taihuai to four hours by car, while a new provincial highway has cut travel time from Taihuai to Taiyuan, Shanxi's capital, to less than three hours. This means that it is easier for people from the two main sources of visitors to reach Wutai Shan, yet also means that people do not have to stay as long. The net result is, according to one local travel agent, a significant drop in the number of longer-term visitors, while several local hotel operators complained that although weekend business was strong, weekday demand was quite low, even during the most popular summer months of July and August.

These responses also illustrate a discernible gender gap in visitor intentions. Of the 166 respondents who said their main purpose in visiting was tied to religion, 104 were women, while of the 49 respondents who were visiting as either tourists or on "field trips," 30 were men. Similarly, while 81 of the 92 men interviewed intended to stay for one or two days, 79 of the 123 women interviewed planned to stay at least three days, including 22 who planned to remain for at least 5 days. These statistics are similar to those of Lang, et al. (2005), who surveyed visitors at a Daoist temple in Guangdong and found a majority to be women and relatively few elderly men.

Missing from this data are foreigners, not because they were deliberately excluded but because they are so few in number. Among guesthouse operators and tour guides at Taihuai, there is general agreement that overseas Chinese and tour groups from neighboring Buddhist countries such as South Korea and Japan are far more common than Europeans and Americans. "Americans and foreigners don't like to visit Wutai Shan anymore," said one shopkeeper. "Every year the foreigners (*laowai*) are fewer and fewer." However, unlike others, he did not think the high admission fee (approximately $35) should be accepted as the cause of this decline:

> Nowadays Chinese have to pay the same prices as foreign guests. It isn't like before when you foreigners had to pay more. I know you foreigners have a lot more money than local people, and you earn a lot more, so why don't more foreigners come here? Things are not the same as before, when there were a lot of foreigners. They liked to bargain, if I said "one hundred eighty" they would say, "eighty" and think they were getting a deal! Nowadays there are a lot of Chinese, they don't like to buy anything, they just want to bargain.

This shopkeeper is evoking a time not just before Wutai Shan became a world heritage site but before social reforms made it possible for Chinese to travel in their country and economic changes created a consumer class with the means to do so. He is also remembering a period when Wutai Shan was an attractive destination to European and North American cultural tourists because foreign travel to more desirable places, such as Tibet, was more restricted. In contemporary China, Wutai Shan no longer has this comparative advantage. Not only can foreigners now visit Buddhist destinations in places that seem more "Buddhist-like" (meaning less Chinese) such as Tibet, Yunnan, and Sichuan, but increased access has made Wutai Shan more "Chinese-like" and less attractive to the types of foreigners who tour religious sites under the guise of cultural tourism.

The absence of Europeans and North Americans is indeed quite striking. For example, during a two-week period in and around Taihuai in July 2011, I encountered only six Euro-Americans: two Canadian students from Nanjing, a French couple, and two American backpackers who complained about the admission price. The French couple said they had a hard time understanding much because there were few signs in any language other than Chinese.

"It's okay if you like temples," one of the Canadians said. "But that's about it. The hiking is okay, but it's better in other places."

In summary, this field data suggests that the majority of people who visit Wutai Shan are Han Chinese, most of whom live within a day's drive. The overwhelming majority of these tourists engage in the practice of *baifo*, literally "to pay homage to Buddha," a practice that was politically unthinkable for most citizens of China even a generation ago.

Pilgrimage in Context

Pilgrimage has been practiced by Buddhists, Confucianists, and Daoists for centuries. However, unlike Muslims and Hindus, Chinese Daoists and Buddhists are not required to engage in a pilgrimage. Instead, people have traveled to sacred destinations for a variety of reasons, ranging from state obligations among rulers and contemplative experience for the literati during the dynastic era to everyday concerns such as penance, health, and future prosperity for commoners (Naquin and Yu 1992). What also distinguishes Chinese pilgrimage practices is a common destination, sacred mountains believed to possess a charismatic aura that predates any built space, a perspective that contradicts postmodern assumptions that built space makes a place sacred. This is reflected in the Chinese term for "pilgrimage," *chaoshan jinxiang*, "to bring incense and pay respects to a (sacred) mountain" (shortened to *chaoxiang* to refer to pilgrims) (11–12).

By the Ming Dynasty (1368–1644), four Buddhist mountains had been identified, linked to the four cardinal directions: in the north, Wutai Shan (Shanxi Province); in the west, Emei Shan (Sichuan); in the east, Putao Shan (Zhejiang); and in the south, Jiuhua Shan (Anhui). However, these destinations served different purposes for different groups. The literary elite visited sacred mountains not so much to pray but to appreciate nature and history by experiencing scenic spots (*jingdian*), destinations marked by artists, poets, and former rulers (Nyíri 2006a:12–13). The importance of mountains as destinations is clear in the formal phrase for this early type of cultural tourism, *mingshan shengdi*, famous mountains and great places. For centuries, devout lay people have visited sacred mountains for reasons of health, penance, and prosperity, while Tibetan Buddhist monks and nuns have done so to pray and make merit. In contrast, Chan (Zen) Buddhist monks historically were not supposed to engage in a pilgrimage to a sacred site but instead to wander between these sites. This idealized notion of a wandering monk has reemerged in the last two decades as state control over mobility has decreased. Thus, for example, in the summer months at Wutai Shan, the population of monks, both Chinese and Tibetan, is at least twice as high as official totals. The official number of monks is based on those registered at temples and monasteries. These monks are considered by authorities as in effect employees of whichever site they are registered. They receive a monthly salary and in return are legally allowed to live at Wutai Shan (although the majority of all legally registered monks leave during the winter months and move to affiliated monasteries and temples in the south, primarily Fujian and Guangdong Provinces). Unofficial monks, in contrast, while not technically legal, are largely tolerated by authorities. Much like the broader migrant labor population, the control of unaffiliated and unregistered religious practitioners has broken down in the last two decades. New forms of travel (such as private bus companies), relaxations on state control of hotels and guesthouses, and the inability of authorities to manage the movement, let alone stop the flow, of enormous numbers of citizens, have contributed to the reemergence of this wandering class of both Daoist priests and Buddhist monks. The net result is that it is far easier to become an unaffiliated Buddhist monk than it is, ironically, to become a tour guide who explains practices at temples and monasteries. To become a licensed tour guide a person must pass a set of rigorous, fact- and statement-based examinations, but to become a monk or a nun requires no more than shaving one's head and buying the required shoes and robes, widely available in local shops in Taihuai.

The key governmental concern with religious practitioners is political: as long as they avoid political issues, they are largely left alone. A case in point is the saga of spiritual movements in the early 1990s that were loosely affiliated with Buddhism such as Zhong Gong and Falun Gong. At their height, these groups attracted millions of followers and generated enormous sums of money but were banned and suppressed when they were perceived to threaten the interests and paramount role of the Communist Party. Indeed, Buddhism in general and Tibetan Buddhism in particular have boomed in recent years, both in rural and urban areas.

In urban bookstores, religious publications ranging from Buddhist and Daoist classics to spiritual guides by prominent monks are almost as numerous as titles in the rapidly expanding field of self-help and self-development, which promise their readers efficient ways of raising personal *suzhi*. Meanwhile, a "Tibet craze" (*xizang*) that began in the years after 1989 shows no sign of slowing. Tibet as a symbol for simplicity, nature, and folk wisdom serves as a backdrop for advertisers selling beer, bottled water, and healthy foods, while Han musicians and artists reproduce these images in their work. Tibet-themed shops sell generically ethnic jewelry, clothing, and handbags in upscale shopping areas of Beijing, Shanghai, and other cosmopolitan cities. After the completion of a rail link to Lhasa in 2006, tourist arrivals doubled to four million in 2007 before dropping almost 50% after ethnic riots in 2008. However, total arrivals reached almost seven million by 2010, and plans call for fifteen million arrivals by 2015. In Lhasa, what had been a foreign backpackers quarter in the old town has become in recent years a largely Han Chinese backpackers ghetto, where young people can go and experience foreignness within the PRC. In short, Tibet, Tibetans, and by extension Tibetan Buddhism have undergone a subtle transformation in popular Han Chinese culture.

On an afternoon train from Beijing to a rail station near Wutai, I experienced this reimagining of Tibet and Tibetans. I found myself sharing a four person "soft" class compartment with a middle-aged man who chain smoked, used his cell phone constantly, and turned out to be a police officer, traveling not to Wutai Shan but to Taiyuan, the provincial capital. Shortly after we departed from the Beijing West Rail Station, a conductor came into our compartment, apologized profusely to my companion while ignoring me, and asked if he minded sharing the space with two Tibetan women. The cop said it was no problem, after which two elderly ladies were escorted in by their sons. They were Khampa from northern Sichuan, and the men were tall, with long hair, cowboy hats, and heavy turquoise jewelry. The two ladies pretended not to understand the police officer's questions to them in Chinese, instead turning their prayer wheels and murmuring quietly. The two sons took up positions in the hallway of our car, where they sat on the floor, smoked, and held court with inquisitive Han passengers. They announced they were accompanying their mothers on a pilgrimage (*chou xiang*) to Wutai

Shan. Chinese passengers quizzed them about Tibetan food, medicines, and praying practices. These were not, however, questions that poked fun or aimed to demonstrate Tibetan backwardness; they centered on, broadly speaking, *weisheng* (the guarding of life) and Chinese assumptions that Tibetans possess secret insights to this. Even the police officer asked questions, and after some time, the elderly ladies also deigned to answer. What was most interesting about this event was the underlying tone: people wanted to experience the assumed aura of these Tibetan pilgrims; the idea of developing or modernizing Tibetans never came up. A popular assumption that Tibetans are simple and unsophisticated no longer is taken as a detriment, but as an exotic quality.

While the reimagining of Tibet and Tibetans within popular Han Chinese culture as simultaneously simple and mystical might appear to be a domestication of popular Euro-American stereotypes about Tibet, it also reflects a historical tradition that links Tibet with China religiously and culturally (Tuttle 2005:222). It is also a very different set of stereotypes than those commonly evoked during the era of High Socialism, when the Party and the State blamed feudal superstitions for Tibet's underdevelopment and declared that Han Chinese had the duty to modernize Tibetans. Finally, this reflects an emerging industry of self-help gurus and spiritual advisors, offering Buddhist and Daoist insights into everything from family questions and how to be ethical in a competitive market society to succeeding in this very type of society. What is striking is how gendered the audience is for these teachers. For example, in the evenings in Taihuai, a common sight in local restaurants is a Han Chinese woman or small group of women eating or drinking tea with an advisor monk, often a Tibetan. One evening I sat beside a woman from Harbin, in Northeastern China, and a young Tibetan monk. She drank tea while he ate a hearty meal of three dishes and discoursed on life's purpose, selflessness, and why desiring (*xiang*) or wanting (*yao*) are futile, except as vows (*yuanwang*) made before Buddha. While the woman was paying the bill, the monk turned around and said hello.

"Are you here to *baifo*?" he asked me.

When I confessed that I wasn't but to learn about developments at Wutai Shan, he pulled out his name card.

"If you ever want to study, email me," he said, handing me a glossy, multicolored card. The front portrayed him superimposed on a backdrop of Gerdeng, the largest Tibetan monastery in Sichuan province; listed his cell phone number; and provided his hotmail email address. The back told his life story in Chinese:

> Lama XXX was born in September 1984 and became a monk in 1995 after being found by searching monks. He studied for five years with a

> famous old Lama named __, who taught him sacred Buddhist scriptures. After finishing first in his class, he enrolled in the Buddhist Studies Institute in Ganze [a Tibetan town in Northern Sichuan] where he studied with another famous Lama. Lama XXX is now in charge of fundraising for a famous temple at Yala Shan (Mount Yala, Sichuan]. He is also available to answer your spiritual questions.

The most visibly pious visitors at Wutai are elderly Han women, who usually travel in tour groups or with a few friends. A boisterous group of retired state employees from Zhejiang was typical. They had flown to Taiyuan, the provincial capital, and then had traveled to the area by tour bus. Their trip would last seven days, all spent in the valley. Besides visiting the main temples around Taihuai, they were completing the traditional pilgrimage to the five peaks, albeit by modern means: rather than walking to each peak, they were reaching each by their bus. Their tour was similar to that of another group I encountered, eleven Tibetan women from the Lhasa region. They, too, had flown to Taiyuan and were going to continue their tour to Beijing, where they intended to do more conventional sightseeing.

On one trip to Wutai from Beijing by public bus, I sat behind two elderly women. When they determined that I could "talk" (*hui shuo*), they told me their life stories. Both retired, Mrs. Li was a widow who had spent most of her life as an office assistant in a public utility work unit where her friend Mrs. Chen had worked as a shop clerk. Born shortly before Liberation (1949), they had lived through the optimism of the Fifties, been caught up in the chaos of the Sixties, endured the deprivation of the Seventies, and survived the wrenching changes of the market reforms of the Nineties. They had also dabbled in *qi gong* and related practices ("But not Falungong!" Mrs. Chen said) and now had embraced mainstream Buddhism. This was their first trip to Wutai Shan, and Mrs. Li was almost giddy with excitement.

Just before our bus reached the south gate to the park entrance, Mrs. Chen consulted with the bus conductor and locked herself in a small box-like restroom in the rear. There were only seven other people on this early summer, late afternoon ride, a group of five college-aged students and a young couple. At the gate, the college students disembarked, gathered their luggage, and disappeared into the night, while the young couple, Mrs. Li and myself were directed to the ticket counter where we each paid our 218 yuan ($34) admission fee to the park and access to the "green" public bus system (as previously noted, green in color but not in effect). We were then led to a metal turnstile. A man in uniform scanned our tickets and officially admitted us, after which we walked through the turnstile and reboarded our bus. A few minutes down the road, we came to a second ticket check gate, where we stopped briefly while another uniformed man boarded and checked each of our tickets. Finally, once past this checkpoint, Mrs. Chen emerged from her cubicle and rejoined her friend, as if nothing out of the ordinary had happened.

This willingness of relative strangers such as our conductor and driver to tolerate what is technically law-breaking is indicative of both the vibrancy of and limits to what is usually referred to in the literature as civil society. As with local residents' responses to regulations and plans that negatively impact their lives, state pricing regulations that make a visit to this mountain area prohibitively expensive for many Chinese citizens are not contested openly or collectively but instead are worked around in a collaborative way. The college-aged students who disembarked at the entrance gate planned to stay at a cheap guesthouse outside the park system and hike around the gate and into the park early in the morning, while Mrs. Chen thought paying more than 200 yuan before spending money for incense and other activities was simply too much money. This leakage in ticket income is reflected in the widely varying estimates of total visitors to Wutai Shan. According to a local administrator in the county-level cultural heritage office, between 300,000 and 400,000 people visited in 2009, while the official figures puts the total at more than 1 million. In short, as with so many aspects of everyday life in contemporary China, significant numbers of people do not openly contest structures and regulations but simply try to "game" the system whenever they can.

Finally, other women travel to Wutai Shan to spend a few days in retreat at a temple or monastery with a master (*shifu*) or at the newly built Buddhist Studies Institute. Several monks confirmed that the vast majority of these short-term students are women, although not just from mainland China. Ms. Lin and her two companions, all from Taiwan, are examples of these overseas Chinese students.

Ms. Lin was middle-aged but in vigorous good health. She and her companions were returning to Beijing after spending a week at a secluded monastery outside of town. She worked with a sex trafficking NGO in Taipei and her friends were teachers. This was her first visit to Wutai Shan. To my question of why they had traveled to Wutai Shan, her response was unequivocal:

> We are not tourists, we are here for meditation and to learn from our *shifu*. Do you know *shifu*? That's "master" in English. These people here [domestic Chinese], they are tourists. They don't know how to *baifo* (worship). All they do is come and ask for things, money or jobs or good luck. That isn't real Buddhism, so they are not really Buddhists.

Although they had to return to Beijing to catch a flight to Taipei, Ms. Lin said she would certainly return to Wutai Shan as soon as she had time.

"My master, he said I should become a nun!" She laughed, perhaps in embarrassment. "He thinks I know enough and have the right desire to be a nun." She had traveled as a tourist just once in China and did not enjoy the experience, citing the crowds, the competition, the noise, and the constant haggling over prices. "I am Chinese," she said. "But I live in Taiwan. I don't like the Communist Party. They aren't even communists! All they care about is money!"

Jifu Temple, near the northern edge of Taihuai, is one of the lesser-visited sites in the area. During summer months, it has between seventy and eighty nuns in residence. Although built during the Qing Dynasty, Jifu Temple has undergone a significant building boom in the last few years, including a new central hall and two multistory wings of single rooms for residents. All of the construction costs have been paid for by private donations, mainly from domestic Chinese. I met one such donor while chatting with a nun about the temple. Another more senior nun walked by with a middle-aged woman. They chatted with me awhile in Chinese, asking standard questions about where I had come from, where I lived, was I alone, and the like. Then the older nun urged the woman to speak English to me because, apparently, she could. Mrs. Qi began not with a set sentence from a textbook but more directly, declaring, "I don't like America." This was not, she explained, because of American military intervention in the Middle East or perceived U.S. government biases against China (common complaints among many Chinese) but because "Americans are too . . . I don't know the word in English . . . too *ziren* (selfish)." You mean the government, I asked? "No," she said emphatically, "Americans."

> It's bad there, really bad. I know because I have been there. *Tamen dou ziren* (they all are selfish). Why is that? Because of capitalism. They worship money (*baiqian*) not Buddha (*baifo*). Most people are Christian, yes or no? Is it okay for Christians to worship money? And now they want the whole world to do the same.

Mrs. Qi lived in Shenzhen, ground zero of the Chinese experiment with capitalism after 1979, when what had been a small village near the border with Hong Kong was transformed into the country's first special economic zone (SEZ) designed to enable the state and private capital to extract value from peasants remade into low-wage factory workers. Shenzhen today is one of the fastest growing cities in the world, with 14 million residents and a reputation as a center of innovation (according to government statistics, one in five of China's doctorate holders live in the city). In addition to its boomtown reputation, skyscrapers, and wealth, Shenzhen has a grittier side, a vast sex industry, loose labor regulations, a large floating population of peasant migrant workers, and stark income disparities. Mrs. Qi owned a textile factory with her husband, traveled widely in China for business, and was wealthy enough to have two children, both of whom studied English with a private American teacher. She was clearly one of the winners in the competitive jungle of "reform and open up," the Party's official description of its ruling policies. In colloquial Chinese, this reform is commonly referred to as "jumping into the sea" (*xiahai*) of the private market, the implication of the metaphor being some will swim and float to the top while others inevitably sink. Yet, despite having risen to the surface, Mrs. Qi also resented what China has become, an ostensibly socialist society in which *ren chi ren* (literally "people eat people," equivalent to "dog eat dog") dominates. Wutai Shan, she told me, was different. "Everyone worships Buddha here," she said, "this is nothing like other places. Here people are honest." She had arrived at Jifu Temple the evening before and was departing later that day for Taiyuan, the provincial capital, where she had business. "I'm busy, always moving, I have to be!" she exclaimed. "But I try to come here when I have time. It's peaceful here, people are kind, so I try to come every chance I can." But she was also not just another quasi-pilgrim, as demonstrated by the treatment she received by the nuns, who were clearly grateful for her financial support. In this sense, she was not just dropping by for spiritual reasons, but also for a different sort of business reason, to check up on her spiritual investment.

Investigation as Tourism

The practice of *kaocha*, literally "on the spot field investigations," is a linguistic holdover from the time of High Socialism, when Party officials at various bureaucratic levels would travel to the field to hear from the grassroots and learn from personal experience the actual impact of state policies. In the new China of socialism with Chinese characteristics, *kaocha* has taken on a new meaning, describing travel junkets to interesting destinations under the guise of official travel. These trips usually involve members of one state entity traveling on state money to a destination where they stay at another state-funded entity. The net result is a dizzying flow of state money from one part of the state to another, or several.

Mr. Peng, a gregarious Cantonese-speaker from Guangdong, looked twenty-two but was thirty-six and worked as a manager in a city land office. He had just arrived at Wutai Shan with a group of his colleagues when I met him in the lobby of one of the mountain villas (*shanzhuang*), moderately upscale hotels that line the route out of the valley to the western peak. This hotel was a joint venture between a businessman from Taiyuan and the county government. They were on a company trip, Peng explained, using the term *danwei* (state enterprise or work unit) rather than *gongsi* (private company). When I asked if he was on vacation, he said this was a *kaocha fangjia*, an "investigation holiday." All expenses were covered by the public (*gongfei*) not by the employees. They had just traveled by bus from Inner Mongolia where they had spent the previous afternoon riding horses.

"That was great!" he said. "You should try it!"

What would they do at Wutai Shan, I asked. *Baifo*?

He laughed slightly. "Maybe the others," he said. "I'm just here to sightsee." When I suggested there was not much to see in the area besides temples, he readily agreed. "It's only for a day," he said. "We leave tomorrow for Taiyuan."

At an overlook high on Dailuo Terrace, I met Wang Xiaohong, a gregarious woman wearing a wide-brimmed hat, oversized sunglasses, and high heels that looked more suitable for a city office than a Buddhist temple on the side of a mountain. She was, she explained, a television producer from Yunnan. She was not, however, in the area to film but for, she said vaguely, a meeting. What sort of meeting, I wondered?

"A seminar," she said. "It is about challenges and opportunities. Our entire office is here." Oh, I replied, assuming this was a seminar on how to portray religion on television. She looked confused.

> Why would it be about religion? Oh, you mean because we are here! No, this seemed an interesting place. I'm not sure why we came here this year. Last summer we went to Hainan Island. I haven't been here before. The weather is nice, but the food isn't very good. And visiting these temples, well, I suppose for good luck it can't hurt.

This type of response, of slight embarrassment and allusions to luck, was a common reaction by state employees on junkets disguised as meetings. While, as survey and interview data suggests, the majority of tourists appear to have some sort of religious intentions, state employees on paid trips are a visible exception. This is in part because of the cost of visiting and in part because of broader state policies. Given the admission fees for Wutai Shan (654 yuan for a family of three, approximately $100), casual visitors whose main motivation is sightseeing are increasingly rare, other than people such as Peng and Wang, whose travel costs were at public expense. Even for middle-class visitors from Beijing, where average family incomes are among the highest in China, admission costs to Wutai Shan for a family of three are prohibitive. Using the Beijing Bureau of Statistic's official family income average of 64,000 yuan as a benchmark, a family trip for three people would cost more than1% of annual income just for admission (*China Daily* 2011). This is comparable to an American family of three, where average family income in 2010 was approximately $46,000, spending almost $500 to enter a national park.

People who visit a site such as Wutai Shan as either self-identified pilgrims or as tourists whose purpose is to worship Buddha are logically more inclined to continue to visit despite the high admission fee. As the cost of admission has risen, first to 90 yuan in 2004 and then to 168 yuan in 2007, the percentage of overall visitors who do not intend to worship has fallen, which suggests the actual annual arrival numbers are much closer to local estimates than to the official numbers issued by the Ministry of Culture. As destination sites such as Wutai Shan have become too expensive for casual visitors, state-affiliated companies, bureaucracies, and other organizations are pressured to not only visit state-affiliated sites but also use state travel agencies, stay in state-affiliated hotels, and even eat in state-linked restaurants. The impact these tourists have on the local economy is consequently quite minimal because the average stay is seldom more than one evening in Taihuai and they spend almost nothing in local shops and restaurants.

Men with Ambiguous Intentions

Besides groups of women with explicit religious intentions and state-affiliated employees on junkets disguised as field trips, a third type of visitor is small groups of men, surprisingly young and often relatively affluent. They travel to Wutai Shan not as self-identified pilgrims or even as worshippers but as seekers of good fortune. One Friday evening, an amiable man named Wu introduced himself in a small shop after his companions insisted he should speak English to me. They were a foursome who had just driven down from Beijing for the night. Former college classmates at a Beijing area university, they all had well paying jobs in the city. Wu sold real estate, Li worked in sales, Ma was a software programmer, and Liu worked for a Hong Kong joint venture. While none appeared to be particularly religious, they had decided to visit for a day because it was the first day of the lunar month and, according to Wu, a "lucky day" for visiting Buddhist temples. Their plan was to spend the night at a cheap guesthouse, tour the main temples the following morning, and then return to Beijing. Were they touring (*lü you*), I asked?

Li: This isn't tourism.
Wu: No, it isn't tourism.
Ma: Well it is, I mean . . . We aren't on vacation (*shujia*) but . . .
RS: Are you guys on a pilgrimage?
Wu: Pilgrimage? Wah, no way! That's what old ladies do!
Li: This is just a day off (*fangjia*). And today is an auspicious day.
RS: Will you burn incense?
Li: Of course, that's what people do in a temple.

RS: So would you say you are here to worship (*baifo*)?
Wu: *Baifo* is *baifo*, that's the point of going to a temple, isn't it? But I'm not a Buddhist. This is a famous scenic spot.
Li: And it's the first day of the month, the time people should visit a temple.

Besides young professionals, another noticeable group of men often seen around temples, especially around the first of the month, are what Chinese call *liumang*, usually translated as "hooligans." These are men who appear to be involved in shady affairs. They wear jewelry, have tattoos, travel in groups, and sprinkle their speech with obscenities that typically refer to someone's mother. However, unlike urban professionals, they readily agree that their purpose is to *baifo*—not for strictly religious reasons but primarily to evoke good luck. This does not preclude them from eating, drinking, smoking and carousing in town if they spend a night.

What to make of these visitors? How to classify them within the standard categories of traveler and tourist, pilgrim and other? Or should they even be classified? There is a growing consensus within the tourism literature that attempts to distinguish between travelers and tourists is a by-product of an idealized notion of what a tourist should do, think, and seek. Thus, for people who travel to a place or places on trips that take them outside of their everyday experiences and routines, a continuum of motives, goals, and inclinations can be identified. It is helpful to label the two points on this continuum as "tourist" and "traveler" and to assign these extreme positions all of the characteristics associated with the cruder forms of each: on one hand, a passive, compliant package tourist who seeks an escape from the everyday routines of life through pure sensory emersion and, on the other hand, a solitary wanderer who seeks if not the meaning of life than the essence of herself by consciously striving to find herself among strangers. Between these two extremes most traveling-tourists can be placed.

Religiously motivated pilgrimage-like travel, however, raises the familiar question of the sacred in contrast to the secular or profane travel of vacationers. This distinction has also been widely critiqued within the literature, and many researchers have concluded that religious pilgrimage is indeed simply a form of tourism. Defining pilgrimage as a journey to a specific destination that evokes particular feelings, some now argue that a journey to places such as Disney World, Graceland, or the Louvre can be just as much a pilgrimage as a journey to Varanasi, the Vatican, or in this case, Wutai Shan. This all depends, according to this view, on the feelings and motivations of individual travelers. One could, I suppose, use a continuum to describe this concept, placing Haj pilgrims to Mecca at one extreme and, say, Elvis fans at the other, and then cheerfully categorizing all possible pilgrim-like travelers in between.

This may make sense in theory, but in practice several questions remain. First of all, the entire debate is an exercise in universal idealism and completely ignores the practical fact that how and why people travel is not simply a product of individual desires but of cultural frames of reference. Tibetans and Mongolians who travel to Wutai Shan as an act of devotion are not on vacation. Nor are young professionals from Beijing who do not want to categorize themselves as either pilgrims or worshippers. The seemingly endless debate about the differences between travel and tourism is rooted in profoundly cultural perceptions about the relationship of individuals to society, the meaning of art, the place of people in nature, and the notion that a distinct "self" exists within each of us that is not yet fully complete. Thus, the familiar Euro-American idealization of a solitary wanderer in search of this elusive self, a self, however, that is not a Western subject at all, let alone a universal one, but a product of an implicit set of reasons and values for traveling that cosmopolitan transnational elites share. Just as behavioral economists declare that all people everywhere are supposed to be naturally motivated by personal gain or loss, despite how real people behave, a long-standing perspective within tourism studies has assumed that "travelers" who seek to engage with themselves through engaging with radical otherness have a more "authentic" experience than tourists. Yet the postmodern solution to this fictive dichotomy (to erase all distinctions) is particularly problematic when examining religious destinations; conflating the categories of "tourism" with "pilgrimage" works only if distinctions between sacred and profane and faith-driven and secular travel are ignored.

Wutai Shan is a world heritage site visited overwhelmingly by a particular type of tourist: cultural-embedded subjects of societies in which Buddhism has had a foundational role in identity formation for centuries. Within this group, the vast majority of these visitors are Chinese, largely domestic but including members of the Chinese Diaspora. This illustrates the resurgent role of Buddhism, both as a religious faith and as a cultural phenomenon, in China over the last two decades, especially in urban areas. As residents have grappled with a radical transformation of lived experiences, ranging from officially approved as well as unofficially tolerated personal values to choices in jobs, education, housing, and even personal relationships, religious practices have gained in popularity (Roberts 2008; Kleinman 2010). However, this renewed interest is easily overlooked if religious *identity* is conflated with religious *practice*. Though Chinese increasingly identify with having faith (*you xinyang*), they are much less likely to foreground possessing religion (*shi zongjiao*) as a key part of their lives.

For example, drawing on survey data collected in six Chinese cities in 1995 and 2005, Yao (2007) reports that only a small percentage of respondents (3.6% in 1995, 5.3% in 2005) self-identified as “religious’ (Yao 2007:174). Yet a majority of those surveyed in 1995 believed in fate and fortune (57.7%), and a similar number engaged in religious practices such as burning paper money and worshipping ancestors (53.9%). In the 2005 survey, while just 2.6% of respondents identified as Buddhists, 14.8% of all respondents kept an image of Buddha at home, 23.1% had worshipped at a Buddhist temple in the previous year, and 77.2% agreed with the fundamental Buddhist precept that “goodness will have good recompense” 176–178). In other words, while religion as an exclusive or primary identity marker is quite low among Han Chinese, religious practice, especially Buddhism, is increasingly important and common.

This is quite visible at the temples at Wutai Shan, where most visitors are Chinese citizens who burn incense, pay homage (*baifo*), and pray (see Figure 5.1). This does not necessarily mean that visitors identify as religious in terms of personal identity because being religious is itself a culturally driven concept. In China, specific ways of being religious exist, such as joining a religious order, recognized religious sect, or association. Unlike among, say, American Christians, religious affiliation and religious practice (belonging and believing) in China, particularly for Buddhists, are not linked. Indeed, the fact that many temple visitors at

Figure 5.1 Tourists burning incense, Wuye Temple, Taihuai: Public worship is the most common activity among visitors to Wutai Shan.

Wutai Shan are not regular practitioners is clear because in several temples lay staff show people how to burn incense and how to bow, while local guidebooks provide detailed images and step-by-step pointers (cf. Su 2006).

However, these temples are not necessarily training sites for instructing people in "how to be Buddhists." Visitors who self-identify as belonging to Buddhism, of having faith (*xinyang*), do not need such instruction, while those who worship the Buddha (*baifo*) when visiting these temples are situational practitioners, concerned with fate and fortune. That is to say, Buddhist temples at Wutai Shan have returned to the pragmatic position they previously occupied in a society that for thousands of years has been pragmatic and inclusive in terms of spiritual belief.

This appears to be the primary motivation for why people visit, be they Tibetan, Han Chinese, Mongolian, Taiwanese, Japanese, Korean, or members of the Chinese Diaspora. The vast majority of visitors are not pilgrims. But nor do they visit for the fresh air, or comfortable climate, or chance to engage with nature. Wutai Shan is a tourist attraction because it has been marked as sacred space for centuries. It is sacred not because visitors feel it has a special meaning but because it is associated with a supernatural aura. In other words, there *is* a distinction between Graceland and Wutai Shan; the former may be a shrine for particularly devout Elvis fans, but the latter has been a source of spiritual insight for centuries.

If most visitors to Wutai Shan have worship intentions, are they therefore on a pilgrimage? Relatively few participate in formal pilgrimage circuits to the five peaks and designated sites along the way, which can take as long as two weeks to complete on foot. Some visitors cover these traditional routes by car or tour bus or spend a few days or more in a monastery guesthouse, either alone or with family or friends. A few wealthy visitors fund private prayer services through generous donations or purchase the counsel of eminent monks. Most visitors arrive by car or tour bus and stay for two or three days. They tour the major sites in groups led by state-licensed guides, and in the evenings eat, drink, or visit cultural performances such as Shanxi Opera. However, what links all of these different forms of practice is the central role of *baifo*: in one way or another most visitors engage in worship. While not identifying as either pilgrims or religious adherents, they engage in pilgrimage-like religious experiences.

With the reemergence of a priest and patron relationship between Buddhist monks and the new elite of urban China has come a reappropriation of the language of faith previously seized upon by the Communist Party during the decades of High Socialism (1957–1979). In its efforts to induce citizens to speak the language of a new and revolutionary society, the CCP promoted the term *shifu*, master, previously used in the sense of the English-appropriated Hindi term *guru*, as the preferred honorific for all male workers, just as terms of hierarchical distinction such as *xiaojie* (Miss), *taitai* (Mrs.), and *xiansheng* (Mr.) were displaced by the all-encompassing *tongzhi* (comrade). But today's China is a very different place, a society betwixt and between capitalism and socialism, one in which the moral framework of selfless worker is for losers while big shots (*da kwan*) and those who are connected call the shots. In this morally ambiguous terrain, one in which a good citizen supposedly serves the people by getting rich, *shifu* once again is used to refer to a religious teacher, one that can be, if not bought, then validated through the market process; *xiaojie* is common slang for a prostitute; and *tongzhi* has been appropriated by the gay community.

AUTHENTICATING A HERITAGE SITE

Little actual preservation, at least in the restorative sense of this term as used by preservationists, is part of the built environment at Wutai, except in one case. This site, however, has nothing to do with Buddhism. In the interior of the Tayuan temple complex is a small *siheyuan*, a traditional courtyard residence. On March 23, 1948, as the People's Liberation Army mounted its final northern offensives against the Republican Government, Mao Zedong and his staff spent one night at Taihuai while traveling through Shanxi province. That evening Mao and his chief deputy Zhou Enlai slept in separate rooms in the courtyard. According to the official Party narrative, the Chairman was impressed enough by his experience to write a brief line commemorating his visit. In this he alluded to local military actions communist guerilla fighters carried out against the Japanese during the 1937–1945 War and Wutai's importance as a base area. "From the establishment of Shanxi's Wutaishan to the establishment of all of China's Wutaishan," Mao wrote, "we fight on to the final victory."

This courtyard, now a memorial site to Mao's visit, has provoked the ire of some foreign visitors. For example, the authors of *The Rough Guide to China* complain that its location "at the heart of one of Buddhism's most sacred sights [sic] is in decidedly poor taste" (Leffman and Zatco 2011:685). Tayuan Temple, while an iconic image of Mount Wutai, is certainly not one of the most sacred destinations in the world for all Buddhists. It was once part of the much older Xiantong temple and was separated in the fifteenth century. Its most famous feature, a large white stupa (pagoda), was designed and built in the early-fourteenth century by a Nepalese architect from the Kathmandu valley. The courtyard memorial to Mao was not randomly placed in this temple to insult Buddhism. This is instead an attempt to frame a different sought of charismatic power, that of revolution.

Shortly after 1949, the Mao-themed courtyard became one of a long list of official destinations in a revolutionary holy land (*geming shengdi*) of communist historical sites (Rioux 2010:83). Rather than banning tourism and pilgrimage to Wutai, the Communist Party attempted to redefine the mountain as a revolutionary tourist attraction, similar to how it aimed to capture the aura of other sacred mountains. Thus, for example, Taishan in Shandong province, the oldest and most sacred of China's holy mountains, is best known for its importance as a site of imperial worship as long ago as the Zhou Dynasty (approximately 1,000 BCE). Following 1949, however, the CCP promoted Taishan as a pilgrimage destination to the tombs of Fan Mingshu, a May 4th activist, and Feng Yuxiang, a warlord who fought against Japanese forces in the 1930s and 1940s (Dott 2010:30).

The courtyard at Tayuan is framed as a sacred site, yet one that is eerily quiet. This Mao memorial is usually empty, despite the nominal two yuan entrance fee (Figure 5.2). Some of the few groups who do visit are government employees on state-sponsored tours. The first thing a visitor encounters after entering is a spirit screen (*zhaobi*), an outer wall designed to provide privacy and block the entrance of evil spirits and ghosts. This spirit screen does not depict dragons or symbols of

Figure 5.2 Entrance to Mao Memorial, Tayuan Temple.

good fortune, however. Its south side is inscribed with Mao's quotation about Wutaishan, while its northern-facing side is covered with a blown up grainy black and white photograph of Mao and Zhou Enlai at the temple.

The north facing rooms in the interior of the courtyard have been carefully preserved (Figure 5.3). A center room serves as a small museum and prayer hall. Officially entitled the "Chairman Mao Resting Hall" (*Mao Zhuxi Lujuguan*), it displays a white bust of Mao surrounded by plastic flowers, with a pillow in front for people to kneel and show their reverence—to *bai* (worship) Mao in place of *Fo* (Buddha). The complete absence of such worshippers is all the more striking given the clatter and chatter of pilgrims and tourists just outside the courtyard as they circle the White Pagoda, turning prayer wheels, chanting, burning incense, taking photographs, listening to tour guides compete with each other's portable loudspeakers, jostling on busy days, an atmosphere thick with the "hotness" and liveliness communicated by the Chinese term *renao*, in contrast to the stillness of the museum-like atmosphere of the Mao memorial hall.

This hall is flanked by two smaller rooms facing east and west and protected by glass (Figure 5.4). Each contains a simple wooden desk and

Figure 5.3 Worshipping the Chairman: A seldom used place for tourists to offer incense to Mao Zedong's memory, Tayuan Temple.

Figure 5.4 Mao slept here: The room where Chairman Mao stayed while spending an evening at Wutai Shan in 1948.

chair, an oil lamp, and a *kang*, a raised platform bed heated by a fire underneath it. A quilt is folded at the end of each bed, while a teacup rests on each table, along with a fountain pen. "This is exactly how the rooms were when Chairman Mao stayed here," the attendant on duty said. "But it looks like it has been repainted," I pointed out. She smiled. "Yes, but the exact same color!"

This claim, that everything is *exactly as it was* in 1948, is what is most striking about these rooms. Seemingly alone in a world heritage site and national park officially dedicated to the preservation of a material record of more than 1,500 years of Buddhism, this forsaken memorial to one insignificant night in the life of a man who sought to eradicate the weight of history in the name of future revolution, this assertion that "Mao slept here, and nothing has been changed," this alone remains true to this other utopian vision: that everything can remain exactly as it ever was.

Conclusion

A central paradox of the world heritage regime is its reliance on policies that do not support and protect cultural differences but construct sameness. The assumptions embedded in how UNESCO, in coordination with ICOMOS, evaluates world heritage sites illustrates this. Although aimed at preserving cultural diversity in an era of globalization presumed to carry the eminent threat of cultural sameness, UNESCO policies mandate a specific spatial form of preservation that erases existing cultural differences and evokes and promotes spatial uniformity. These policies mandate the separation of material culture deemed to be heritage worthy from the lived spatial practices of cultural subjects. The net result is a labor-intensive dismantling of existing built space that is akin to the construction of zoos and nature parks. Just as some animals are "preserved" by being placed in an (unnatural) environment of "nature" and "nature" itself is preserved by being cordoned off from human society in parks, material culture identified as of global importance is now to be separated from society itself.

This transnational heritage process has not been imposed on a reluctant state in China. As I have argued in this book, for more than a century, the paramount national state objective has been modernization based on an explicit faith in science, technology, and the objectifying gaze of rational action. This strategy has included campaigns to destroy tangible cultural sites and intangible practices during the Cultural Revolution as well as to promote historical sites as world-heritage worthy during the current era. However, this recent shift to heritage preservation has occurred for different reasons, as illustrated in the case of Wutai Shan. For UNESCO authorities, this sacred mountain is to be preserved and protected from negative effects of modernization such as excessive tourism (caused ironically by the material success of the modernization movement in China). This objective is fundamentally at odds with the various objectives of different parts of the Chinese state. The national promotion of heritage is, I have argued, a logical outgrowth of the Communist Party's continued focus on the cultivation of a modern sensibility among citizens. The emphasis on the moral and spiritual aspects of modernity has been a central concern of ruling elites since the late-nineteenth century when Qing reformers began to advocate for a modernization campaign that would be based on the essence of Chinese culture, history, and morals. From this perspective, heritage projects contribute to the Party and (national) State effort to increase both the quality and civility of its citizen-subjects.

However, other parts of the state have their own concerns and objectives. While national-level bureaucrats involved in environmental issues support re-greening this mountainous area, they do not necessarily support policies aimed at increasing tourism. In like manner, local and provincial officials may support the use of Wutai Shan's reputation as a religious destination to promote mass tourism as an economic development tool, while officials involved in cultural heritage preservation at various levels of the government may want limits on visitors. Finally, Party and state bureaucrats charged with monitoring and managing religious practice must grapple with a clear fact: the marketing of Wutai Shan as a national and world heritage site has not resulted in it becoming a destination spot for cultural or green tourists, just as a previous state attempt to remake Ta Yuan Temple as an historical revolutionary pilgrimage destination because of Mao's visit in 1948 did not lead people to view this Buddhist temple as a Party shrine. Instead, the branding of Wutai Shan as a world heritage destination has facilitated its reemergence in the popular consciousness as a sacred space of Buddhist aura and power. Finally, local interests as well are quite diverse: while monastic authorities and monks use tourist visits to raise funds, other local residents seek to make a living off of tourism while grappling with personal displacement. At the local level, the heritage preservation process has resulted in a radical remaking of local landscapes. Rather than simply preserving what exists, these policies have led to visible *destruction* (of local homes, shops, and farm land), *renovation* (of shops and homes not yet demolished), and *construction* (of parkland and visitor facilities but also of new monastic buildings and entire new temples). Taihuai town, located in the center of the new heritage zone, is an example of how state policies have continuously reworked local landscapes since 1949. After liberation, private businesses were abolished and land was redistributed to households. Within a decade households and agricultural land were organized first into collectives and then into communes. Following the 1982 national land reforms, agricultural collectives were abolished and land was redistributed to families. In 1987, rural residents were allowed to run small businesses again, leading to the (re)creation of the local service economy centered on monastic life and visitors that had existed prior to liberation in 1949. But in 2005, following the establishment of Wutai National Park and approval of a master plan for heritage management, residents began to lose their homes, farm land, and businesses to preservation. In the course of three generations, the local landscape was, in turn, nationalized, redistributed, collectivized, privatized, and finally (re)collectivized, not however in the name of the people but in the name of preservation.

One explanation of this dilemma of displacement would cite the state versus society paradigm often evoked by proponents of civil society development projects. According to this argument, the absence of a civil society in China explains what has happened at Wutai Shan. Recognizing that cultural heritage preservation is a complex process that should involve all residents, local, provincial and national officials, preservationists, and commercial interests requires a civil society framework. Until this emerges, the PRC will continue to be run as a semiauthoritarian state that limits the rights of citizens.

The main problem with this "bad state" versus rights-lacking society framework is that it glosses over the social realities of China. As I have argued, no homogeneous society contests a monolithic state at Wutai Shan because neither exists. An arduous, contentious, and drawn-out process of heritage preservation is in this case indicative of an emerging civil society, not the complete lack of this. In other words, the lack of bureaucratic efficiency in the implementation of state plans and mandates and the complete absence of a uniform oppositional voice are not problems to be fixed but signs of dissent and, at least potentially, dialogue.

In China, the Party-State has guided society on a dizzying modernization drive for two decades, including the development of a widespread heritage industry that includes not just local, provincial, national, and world heritage sites but also cultural theme parks, national parks and forests, and recently constructed historically themed shopping zones in urban areas. Though nonstate actors may not be able to stop or radically alter a heritage plan, they can still have an impact. Indeed, citizen input is, in measured tones, taken seriously by government and Party officials, particularly at the national level.

Rather than a process of saving the past from the ravages of the present or of separating out the real from the fake, heritage preservation should be seen as, in the words of Laurajane Smith, "moments of negotiation" (2007:165). This requires rethinking what we mean by an *in situ* framework for material sites. Rather than abandoning the archeological insistence on proper context and the relative truth of empirical facts, a more holistic *in situ* framework would acknowledge the existence and validity of ongoing social relationships at these sites. Therefore, the social landscape of heritage sites such as Wutai Shan should be recognized and accepted for what they are, as aspects of the social vibrancy of the site itself. Sites such as temples, landscapes, and material objects provide, as Smith points out, a "sense of place" (165). This sense, however, is not transcendentally universal: it is grounded in the lived experiences of particular culturally-embedded actors. This approach stands in sharp contrast to the UNESCO project of monumentalizing world heritage sites as part of its global narrative. This UNESCO project seeks to turn such sites into markers of a world community understandable to all (Di Giovine 2009:86–89). It also differs from how world heritage is currently constructed in the PRC, not as tangible parts of a global cultural order but as world-class *Chinese* heritage sites.

On my last trip to Wutai Shan I hiked up to the new Wenshu Temple on a clear June morning. Construction on the main hall had been finished and several workers were busy carving the front gate. A lean man in his thirties came over and started talking. Mr. Tang was a mural painter from a small town in Shandong Province who made a living painting Buddhist images. Through a friend, he had been hired to work on this new temple, and had been making regular trips to Wutai for the past two years. When I asked him why he thought so many tourists visited Wutai Shan, Tang looked at me oddly. "Why do people come here? To worship Buddha, of course! Why else? " He then explained how that had been unthinkable before the reform period begun by Deng Xiaoping. But rather than saying that the government or the Party now allowed religious practice, he suggested that the reforms had unleashed the incipient power of Buddhism. This did not need to be relearned, redeveloped, or recultivated; it had remained dormant at the mountain waiting for the moment when the state would recognize this aura.

> Immediately in the years after the reforms began, becoming aware of and feeling (*ganjue*) Pusa [Buddha] became strong again. That's why so many people come here. Pusa is here, did you know that? Yes, this is where Wenshu [Manjusri] is. But after Liberation none of this was possible. Nobody came here, and all the monks went away. No way could I have painted Pusa back then, everything was Chairman Mao. Even when I was studying we were supposed to paint only people like Mao. It was like he was a Buddha! But he's gone now, right? He is in Tiananmen [location of Mao's mausoleum], Wenshu is still here. So worshipping is no problem

> now. The government is building roads to here, so this shows it's okay now, they want people to worship. Why else would this be a world heritage place?

This view, "from another country heard from" (Gerrtz 1973), reminds us that the heritage conversation is not yet finished. In the case of Wutai Shan, world heritage status does not simply symbolize its place within a UNESCO-shaped tangible encyclopedia of world culture, nor its status as a marker of Chinese national heritage. Instead, it signifies recognition of the aura of Wenshu's mountain, the reason why so many come.

Notes

Chapter 1

1. With some exceptions, most notably Shenandoah National Park, established in 1935. The development of the Blue Ridge Mountains into a national park included the removal and forced relocation of several thousand mountain residents.

Chapter 2

1. The first such list, in 1961, included 33 revolutionary sites, 14 grottoes, 11 stone carvings, 19 tombs, 77 buildings, and 26 ancient sites. The expanded 1982 list included 43 revolutionary sites, 19 grottoes, 13 stone carvings, 26 tombs, 105 buildings, and 36 ancient sites (Liu 1983:97).
2. Between 1969 and 1978, millions of urban teenagers were forcibly relocated to rural villages as part of Mao's "Down to the Countryside Movement" (Shangshan Xiacun Yundong). This campaign, ostensibly designed to educate city residents about the realities of China, was also aimed at restoring social stability by removing radical Red Guards from urban areas. Many remained trapped in the countryside for years, especially those who had married.

Chapter 3

1. These four zones are a strict protection zone where construction that threatens the "authenticity of cultural resources" is prohibited, an ecological coordination zone surrounding the core area, a visitor utilization zone, and a community utilization zone ("Conservation and Management Plan for the Nominated World Heritage Site of Mount Wutai," 211).

CHINESE-ENGLISH GLOSSARY

aiguo zhuyi: 爱国者 patriotism

bai: 拜 worship

baifo: 拜佛 to worship Buddha

chai: 拆 to demolish

chaoshan jinxiang: 朝山进香 to bring incense and pay respects to a (sacred) mountain

chaoxiang: 烧香 pilgrim

chengxu: 烧香 social order

chuanlian: 串联 to exchange experiences (Cultural Revolution-era)

da war: 大腕儿 big shot (slang)

danwei: 单位 work unit

daode: 道德 morality

dīngzihù: 钉子户 nail house (signifies a property owner who refuses to move when their home is targeted for demolishment)

fanggu: 仿古 'copies of ancient places' (newly built neighborhoods themed as old)

fangjia: 放假 holiday

fazhan: 发展 development

fengjian mixin: 封建迷信 feudal superstition

Fo: 佛 Buddha

geming shengdi: 革命圣地 'revolutionary holy land'; tourism or heritage destinations connected to recent political history

genzhe ganjue zou: 跟着感觉走 to pursue personal feelings

Gongchangdang: 共产党 Chinese Communist Party (CCP)

gongde: 公德 public morality

gongfei: 公费 at public expense

guanxi: 关系 personal connections or relationships

guofu: 国父 'Father of the country' (Sun Yatsen/Sun Zhongshan)

Guojia Wenwu Chu: 国家文物处 State Administration of Cultural Heritage (SACH), known until 2003 as the "State Cultural Relics Bureau"

Guomin: 国民 citizens

Guomindang: 国民党 Chinese Nationalist Party (KMT)

hexie: 和谐 harmonious

hukou: 户口 residency permit

jilu: 纪律 discipline

jingdian: 景点 scenic spot

jingji fang: 经济房 state-subsidized housing (more formally *jingji shiyong fang* 经济适用房)

jingshen: 精神 spiritual

jingshen wenhua yundong: 精神文化运动 Spiritual Civilization Campaign (1982)

Jinxiu Zhonghua: 景秀中华 Splendid China Theme Park

kang: 炕 raised platform bed

kaocha: 考察 'field inspections' (travel at public expense)

kongqi: 空气 environment

laowai: 老外 foreigner

limao: 礼貌 courtesy, politeness

lixiang: 理想 ideals

liumang: 流氓 hooligan; gangster

luyou: 旅游 travel, tourism

mangliu: 盲流 migrant worker

mixin: 迷信 'blind belief'; superstition

minjian xinyang: 民间信仰 folk practices

minzu: 民族 ethnicity, nationality, race

Minzu Wenhua Cun: 民族文化村 China Folk Culture Village

mingshan shengdi: 名山胜地 famous mountains and great places; shortened to *mingsheng* 名胜

qi: 气 The fundamental energy force of the universe

qidao: 祈祷 'to entreat or beg'; prayer (used with Abrahamic religions)

qiangjian: 强建 'snatch or steal' (*qiang*) and 'construct' (*jian*); used to describe home improvements by property-owners facing displacement as a means of increasing official compensation

renao: 热闹 'hot and noisy'; a fun atmosphere

ren: 仁 one's humaneness; the fundamental Confucian value

ren chi ren: 人吃人 'people eat people', equivalent to 'dog eat dog'

Sanmin Zhuyi: 三民主义 “Three Principles of the People” (Sun Yatsen)

Shanshui: 山水 ‘mountain and water’; Chinese landscape paintings

shangshan xiacun yundong: 上山下乡运动 ‘Down to the Countryside Campaign’ (Cultural Revolution-era resettlement of urban youth in rural areas)

shangpin fang: 商品房 commercial private housing

shaoshu minzu: 少数民族 official minority ethnic group

shifu: 师傅 master

shujia: 暑假 vacation

siheyuan: 四合院 traditional courtyard residence

sixiang zhengzhi gongzuo: 思想政治工作 political thought work

shiye: 失业 unemployed

suyang: 素养 embodied character

suzhi: 素质 quality (of people)

tian ren heyi: 天人合一 the harmony of heaven and people’

tongzhi: 同志 comrade

waidi ren: 外地人 non-local Chinese

waiguo ren: 外国人 foreigner

weisheng: 卫生

hygiene *weixin*: 卫信 temple renewal

wenhua: 文化 culture

wenhua gongcheng: 文化工 cultural engineering

wenming: 文明 civilization, civilized, civility

wenming jingdian: 文明景点 civilized scenic spot

wenming shouze: 文明守则 rules of civilized behavior

Wenshu: 文殊菩萨 Manjusri (Buddha of Wisdom)

Wuzhi: 物质 material (in contast to spiritual, *jingshen*)

Xiahai: 下海 ‘jump into the sea’; to leave state employment

xiandai zhuyi: 现代主义 modernization

xiaojie: 小姐 ‘Miss’; now slang term for a prostitute

xiaokang shehui: 小康社会 a broadly prosperous society

xin shenghuo yundong: 新生活运动 New Life Movement (KMT, 1934-1937)

xinyang: 信仰 faith (contrast with *zongjiao*, religion)

yi: 裔 barbarian; people beyond the frontier (Confucianism)

yiban mixin: 一般迷信 ‘common superstitions’; another term for folk practices

yichan: 遗产 heritage

zhaobi: 照壁 spirit screen

Zhongdian Wenwu Baohu Danwei: 重点文物保护单位 ‘Key Cultural Protection Unit’; national heritage site *zhongguo ren*: 中国人 Chinese person

zhonghua minzu: 中华民族 Chinese nation

zhonghua xiyong: 中华西用 to utilize Western technology, ideas, and products while maintaining a Chinese cultural essence

zhongyang jingshen weming jianshe zhidao weiyuanwei: 中央精神文明建设指导委员会 Central Commission for Building Spiritual Civilization (1997)

ziran: 自然 nature

ziren: 自私 selfish

zizhi: 自制 self-governance

zongjiao: 宗教 religion

zongjiao wenhua luyou: 宗教文化旅游 religious-cultural tourism

References

Adams, Alexander (ed.). *First World Conference on National Parks.* Washington, DC: Department of the Interior and National Park Service, 1962.

Agnew, Neville, and Martha Demas (eds.). *Principles for the Conservation of Heritage Sites in China: English Language Translation, with Chinese Text, of the Document Issued by China ICOMOS.* Los Angeles: The Getty Conservation Institute, 2004 [2002].

Ahmad, Yahaya. "The Scope and Definitions of Heritage: From Tangible to Intangible." *International Journal of Heritage Studies* 12:3 (2006), 292–300.

Anagnost, Ann. "The Politics of Ritual Displacement." In Charles Keyes, Laurel Kendall, and Helen Hardacre (eds.), *Asian Visions of Authority: Religion and the Modern States of East and Southeast Asia* (pp. 221–224). Manoa: University of Hawaii Press, 1994.

——— "The Corporeal Politics of Quality (*Suzhi*)." *Public Culture* 16:2 (Spring 2004), 189–208.

——— *National Past-Times: Narrative, Representation, and Power in China.* Durham, NC: Duke University Press, 1997.

Anderson, Benedict. *Imagined Communities: Reflections on the Origins and Spread of Nationalism.* New York: Verso, 2006 [1983].

Anonymous. "Moving Residents Betrays History." Reprinted in *The Manchester Guardian,* March 13, 2008. Accessed March 3, 2010: http://www.guardian.co.uk/world/2008/mar/13/china?commentpage=1

Ashworth, G. J. "From History to Heritage—From Heritage to Identity." In G. J. Ashworth and P. J. Larkham (eds.), *Building a New Heritage* (pp. 13–30). London: Routledge, 1994.

Badone, Ellen, and Sharon Roseman (eds.). "Introduction." In *Intersecting Journeys: The Anthropology of Pilgrimage and Tourism* (pp. 1–17). Urbana: University of Illinois Press, 2004.

——— *Intersecting Journeys: The Anthropology of Pilgrimage and Tourism.* Urbana: University of Illinois Press, 2004.

Baker, Aryn. "Should Buddhas Blasted by the Taliban be Rebuilt?" *Time*, June 26, 2008. Accessed January 4, 2012: http://www.time.com/time/world/article/0,8599,1818299,00.html

Beltràn, Enrique. "Use and Conservation: Two Conflicting Principles." In Alexander Adams (ed.), *First World Conference on National Parks* (pp. 35–43). Washington, DC: Department of the Interior and National Park Service, 1962.

Blum, Deborah. *Portrait of "Primitives": The Making of Human Kinds in the Chinese Nation*. Lanham, MD: Rowman & Littlefield, 2000.

Branigan, Tania. "Mountain Residents Bulldozed out of Government's World Heritage Vision." *The Manchester Guardian*, March 13, 2008. Accessed February 28, 2010: http://www.guardian.co.uk/world/2008/mar/13/china1

Bray, David. *Social Space and Governance in Urban China*. Palo Alto, CA: Stanford University Press, 2005.

Bremer, Thomas. *Blessed with Tourists: The Borderlands of Religion and Tourism in San Antonio*. Chapel Hill: University of North Carolina Press, 2003.

———"Sacred Spaces and Tourist Places." In Timothy Dallen and Daniel Olsen (eds.), *Tourism, Religion, and Spiritual Journeys* (pp. 25–35). New York: Routledge, 2006.

Brooks, Graham. "The ICOMOS International Cultural Tourism Charter: Linking Cultural Heritage Conservation to the Celebration of Cultural Diversity." In *Estrategias Relativas al Patrimonio Cultural Mundial. La Salvaguarda en un Mundo Globalizado. Principios, Practicas y Perspectivas*. 13th ICOMOS General Assembly and Scientific Symposium. Actas. Comité Nacional Español del ICOMOS, Madrid, 2002, 308–310.

Bruner, Edward. "Science and Humanism in Tourism Studies." *Annals of Tourism Research* 37:3 (2010), 861–865.

"Chairman Mao Reviews a Total of 11 Million of Mighty Cultural Revolution Army." *Peking Review* 9:49 (December 2, 1966), 6–9.

Chang, Maria Hsia. *Falun Gong: The End of Days*. New Haven, CT: Yale University Press, 2004.

Chau, Adam (ed.). *Religion in Contemporary China: Revitalization and Innovation*. London: Routledge, 2011.

Chen, Walter Hanming. "The New Life Movement." Nanjing: Information Bulletin, Council of International Relations, December 31, 1936, 189–230.

China Daily, "Fairer Compensation" (Editorial), June 10, 2011. Accessed July 18, 2011: http://www.chinadaily.com.cn/opinion/2011-06/10/content_12669221.htm

China National Tourism Office (CNTO). "Major Statistics of Domestic Tourism 2007." Accessed October 10, 2011: http://74.125.93.132/search?q=cache:http://www.cnta.gov.cn/html/2008-6/2008-6-2-21-29-3-319.html

———"Major Statistics of Chinese Tourism, January–December 2008." Accessed October 10, 2011: http://www.cnta.gov.cn/html/2009-2/2009-2-18-9-34-95871.html

———"Foreign Visitor Arrivals by Purpose, January–December 2009." Accessed October 12, 2011: http://cnto.org/chinastats_2009ArrivalsByPurpose.asp

Chou Wen-Shing. "Ineffable Paths: Mapping Wutaishan in Qing Dynasty China." *Art Bulletin* 89:1 (2007), 108–129.

Cleere, Henry. "The Uneasy Bedfellows: Universality and Cultural Heritage." In Robert Layton, Peter Stone, and Julian Thomas (eds.), *Destruction and Conservation of Cultural Property* (pp. 22–29). London: Routledge, 2001.

Cohen, Erik. "Pilgrimage and Tourism: Convergence and Divergence." In E. A. Morris (ed.), *Sacred Journeys: The Anthropology of Pilgrimage* (pp. 47–61). Westport, CT: Greenwood Press, 1992a.

———"Pilgrimage Centers: Concentric and Excentric." *Annals of Tourism Research* 19:1 (1992b), 33–50.

Cohen, Michael. *The Pathless Way: John Muir and the American Wilderness*. Madison: University of Wisconsin Press, 1984.

Coleman, Simon, and John Eade. *Pilgrim Voices: Narrative and Authorship in Christian Pilgrimage*. London: Berghahn Books, 2004.

Collins-Kreiner, Noga. "Researching Pilgrimage: Continuity and Transformations." *Annals of Tourism Research* 37:2 (2010), 440–456.

Collins-Kreiner, Noga, and N. Kliot. "Pilgrimage Tourism in the Holy Land: The Behavioral Characteristics of Christian Pilgrims." *GeoJournal* 50:1 (2000), 55–67.

Confucius. *The Analects* (trans. Dawson Raymond). New York: Oxford University Press, 1993.

Denton, Kirk. "Museums, Memorial Sites and Exhibitionary Culture in the People's Republic of China." *The China Quarterly* 183 (September 2005), 565–586.

de Bary, Theodore, and Lufrano, Richard (eds.). *Sources of Chinese Tradition* (Vol. II). New York: Columbia University Press, 2001.

Digance, Justin. "Pilgrimage at Contested Sites." *Annals of Tourism Research* 30:1 (2006), 143–159.

Di Giovine, Michael. *The Heritage-Scape: UNESCO, World Heritage, and Tourism*. Lanham, MD: Lexington Books, 2009.

Dikötter, Frank. *The Discourse of Race in Modern China*. Palo Alto, CA: Stanford University Press, 1992.

——— *Mao's Great Famine: the History of China's Most Devastating Catastrophe, 1958–1962*. New York: Walker and Company, 2010.

Dirlik, Arif. "The Ideological Foundations of the New Life Movement: A Study in Counter-Revolution." *Journal of Asian Studies* 34:4 (1975), 945–980.

Dixon, Bruce. *Red Capitalists in China: The Party, Private Entrepreneurs, and Prospects for Change*. Cambridge, England: Cambridge University Press, 2003.

Dott, Brian. "Spirit Money: Tourism and Pilgrimage on the Sacred Slopes of Mount Tai." In Tim Oakes and Donald Sutton (eds.), *Faiths on Display: Religion, Tourism, and the Chinese State* (pp. 27–49). Lanham, MD: Rowman & Littlefield, 2010.

Dutt, Sagarika (ed.). *UNESCO and a Just World Order*. New York: NOVA Science Publishing, 2002.

Dynon, Nicholas. "Four Civilizations: The Evolution of Post-Mao Chinese Socialist Ideology." *The China Journal* 60 (2008), 83–109.

Eade, John, and Michael Sallnow. *Contesting the Sacred: The Anthropology of Christian Pilgrimage*. London: Routledge, 1991.

The Economist, "Private Property in China: Redevelopment with a Human Face?" January 28, 2011. Accessed July 10, 2011: http://www.economist.com/blogs/banyan/2011/01/private_property_china

Elliot, Robert (ed.). *Environmental Ethics*. Oxford and New York: Oxford University Press, 1995.

Elychar, Julie. *Markets of Dispossession: NGOs, Economic Development and the State in Cairo*. Durham, NC: Duke University Press, 2005.

Engberg, Robert, and Donald Wesling (eds.). *John Muir: To Yosemite and Beyond.* Madison: University of Wisconsin Press, 1980.

Englund, Harri. *Prisoners of Freedom: Human Rights and the African Poor*. Berkeley: University of California Press, 2006.

Erbaugh, Mary. "China Expands its Courtesy: Saying 'Hello' to Strangers." *Journal of Asian Studies* 67:2 (2008), 621–652.

Eriksen, Thomas. "Between Universalism and Relativism: A Critique of the UNESCO Concept of Culture." In Jane Cowen, Marie-Bénédicte Dembour, and Richard Wilson (eds.), *Culture and Rights: Anthropological Perspectives* (pp. 127–148). Cambridge, England: Cambridge University Press 2001.

Errington, Fredrick, and Deborah Gewertz. "Tourism and Anthropology in a Post-Modern World." In Sharon Gmelch (ed.), *Tourists and Tourism* (pp. 91–113). Long Grove, IL: Waveland Press, 2009.

Errington, Sherry. *The Death of Authentic Primitive Art and Other Tales of Progress.* Berkeley: University of California Press, 1998.

Farrer, James. *Opening Up: Youth Sex Culture and Market Reform in Shanghai.* Chicago: University of Chicago Press, 2002.

Ferguson, James. *The Anti-Politics Machine: Development, Depoliticization, and Bureaucratic Power in Lesotho*. Minneapolis: University of Minnesota Press, 1994.

Fischer, Emil. *The Sacred Wutai Shan: In Connection with Modern Travel from Taiyuan Fu via Mount Wutai to the Mongolian Border*. Shanghai: Kelly & Walsh Publishers, 1925.

"Foreign News: Four Virtues." *Time*, October 8, 1934.

Friedman, Sara. "Embodying Civility: Civilizing Processes and Symbolic Citizenship in Southeast China." *Journal of Asian Studies* 63:3 (2004), 687–718.

Gable, Eric, and Richard Handler. "After Authenticity at an American Heritage Site." *American Anthropologist* 98:2 (1998), 568–578.

Gimello, Robert. "Chang Shang-Ying on Wutai Shan." In Susan Naquin and Chun Fang-Yu (eds.), *Pilgrims and Sacred Sites in China* (pp. 89–149). Berkeley: University of California Press, 1992.

Gladney, Dru. *Dislocating China: Muslims, Minorities, and Other Subaltern Subjects.* Chicago: University of Chicago Press, 2004.

Global Heritage Fund (GHF). "Foguang Temple A Tang Dynasty Treasure." Palo Alto, CA, 2009. Accessed January 4, 2012: http://globalheritagefund.org/images/uploads/projects/foguang_2pager.pdf

Government of China (GOC). *Conversation and Management Plan for the Nominated World Heritage Site of Mount Wutai.* Beijing: State Administration of Cultural Heritage, January 2008a.

Government of China (GOC). *Nomination Report for Mount Wutai* (Yang Rui, Editor-in-Chief). Beijing: State Administration of Cultural Heritage, January 2008b.

Government of China (GOC). "State-Owned Land and Compensation Ordinance" [Public Law 590]. Beijing: State Council, January 19, 2011.

Graber, Linda. *Wilderness as Sacred Space.* Washington, DC: American Association of Geographers, 1976.

Graburn, Nelson. "Tourism: The Sacred Journey." In V. L. Smith (ed.), *Hosts and Guests: The Anthropology of Tourism* (pp. 33–47). Philadelphia: University of Pennsylvania Press 1977.

Greenwood, Davydd. "Culture by the Pound: An Anthropological Perspective on Tourism as Cultural Commoditization." In Valene Smith (ed.), *Hosts and*

Guests: The Anthropology of Tourism (pp. 171–186). Philadelphia: University of Pennsylvania Press, 1989 [1977].

Gruber, Stephen. Protecting China's Cultural Heritage Sites in Times of Rapid Change: Current Developments, Practice and Law." *Asia Pacific Journal of Environmental Law* 253:10 (2007), 253–301.

Gu Chaolin, and Shen Jianfa. "Transformation of Urban Socio-Spatial Structure in Socialist Market Economies: The Case of Beijing." *Habitat International* 27 (2003), 107–122.

Han, Feng. "The Chinese View of Nature: Tourism in China's Scenic and Historic Interest Areas." Dissertation, Queensland University of Technology, Queensland, Australia, 2006.

Harrison, Henrietta. *The Making of the Republican Citizen: Political Ceremonies and Symbolism in China 1911–1929*. New York: Oxford University Press, 2000.

Hevia, James. "World Heritage, National Culture, and the Restoration of Chengde." *Positions* 9:1 (2001), 219–243.

Huxley, Julian. *UNESCO: Its Purpose and Philosophy*. Washington, DC: American Council on Public Affairs, 1947.

International Council on Monuments and Sites (ICOMOS). *International Charter for the Conservation and Restoration of Monuments and Sites* (The Venice Charter (2003)). Accessed November 25, 2011: http://www.international.icomos.org/charters/venice_e.htm

Jacka, Tamara. "Cultivating Citizens: Quality (*Suzhi*) Discourse in the PRC." *Positions* 17:3 (2009), 523–535.

Kang Xiaofei. "Two Temples, Three Religions, and a Tourist Attraction: Contesting Sacred Space on China's Ethnic Frontier." *Modern China* 35:3 (2009), 227–255.

Kieschnick, John. *The Impact of Buddhism on Chinese Material Culture*. Princeton, NJ: Princeton University Press, 2003.

Kipnis, Andrew. "Suzhi: A Keyword Approach." *China Quarterly* 2006, 295–313.

———"Neoliberalism Reified: Suzhi Discourse and Tropes of Neoliberalism in the PRC." *Journal of the Royal Anthropological Institute* 13 (2007), 383–400.

Kirby, William. "Engineering China: Birth of the Development State, 1928–1937." In Yeh Win-Hsin (ed.), *Becoming Modern: Passages to Modernity and Beyond* (pp. 137–160). Berkeley: University of California Press, 2000.

Kleinman, A. "Remaking the Moral Person in China." *The Lancet*, 375 (March–April 2010), 1074–1075.

Kohle, Natalie. "Why did the Kangxi Emperor go to Wutai Shan? Patron, Pilgrimage, and the Place of Tibetan Buddhism at the Early Qing Court." *Late Imperial China* 29:1 (June 2008), 73–119.

Lang, Graeme, Selina Ching Chan, and Lars Raguald. "Folk Temples and the Religious Economy." In Fenggang Yang and Joseph B. Tamney (eds.), *State, Market, and Religions in Chinese Societies* (pp. 149–180). Leiden: Brill, 2005.

Laozi. *The Daodejing* (trans. Arthur Waley). Changsha: Hunan People's Press, 1999.

Layton, Robert, Peter Stone, and Julian Thomas (eds.). *Destruction and Conservation of Cultural Property*. London: Routledge, 2001.

Lee Ching Kwan. *Against the Law: Labor Protests in China's Sunbelt and Rustbelt*. Berkeley, University of California Press, 2007.

Lee, Leo Ou-Fan. *Shanghai Modern*. Cambridge, MA: Harvard University Press, 1999.

Lee Yok-Shiu. "The Urban Housing Problem in China." *China Quarterly* 115 (September 1988), 387–407.

Leffman, David, and Martin Zattco. *The Rough Guide to China*. London: Penguin Books, 2011.

Li, Fung Mei, and Trevor Sofield. "Huangshan (Yellow Mountain), China: The Meaning of Harmonious Relationships." In Chris Ryan and Gu Huimin, *Tourism in China: Destinations, Cultures, and Communities* (pp. 157–167). London: Routledge 2009.

Li Jinyu. "The Politics of Propriety: A Comparative Study of the New Life Movement and the Five Stresses and Four Beautifications Campaign in Twentieth century China." Master's thesis, Houston: Rice University, 1987.

Light, Andrew, and Holmes Rolston (eds.). *Environmental Ethics: An Anthology*. Oxford, England: Blackwell Publishers, 2003.

Liu Bai. *Cultural Policy in the People's Republic of China: Letting a Hundred Flowers Bloom*. Paris: UNESCO, 1983.

Logan, William. "Closing Pandora's Box: Human Rights Conundrums in Cultural Heritage Protection." In Helaine Silverman and D. Fairchild Ruggles, *Cultural Heritage and Human Rights* (pp. 33–52). New York: Springer Press, 2007.

Lowenthal, David. "Natural and Cultural Heritage." *International Journal of Heritage Studies* 11:1 (2005), 81–92.

Leung, C. B. "The Transformation of Social Welfare Policy: The Restructuring of the Iron Rice Bowl." In Wen Fangtang and William Parrish, *Chinese Urban Life Under Reform* (pp. 617–643). Cambridge, England: Cambridge University Press, 2000.

Lu Ping. "Beyond Mr. Democracy and Mr. Science: The Introduction of Miss Morals and the Trend of Moral revolution in the New Culture Movement. *Historical China* 2:2 (2007), 254–286.

Lu Xiaobo, and Elizabeth Perry, "Introduction." In Lu and Perry (eds.), *Danwei: The Changing Chinese Workplace in Historical and Comparative Perspective* (pp. 1–20). Armonk, NY: M.E. Sharpe, 1997.

Mackenzie, John. *The Empire of Nature: Hunting, Conservation, and British Imperialism*. Manchester, UK: Manchester University Press, 1988.

MacCannell, Dean. *The Tourist: A New Theory of the Leisure Class*. Berkeley: University of California Press, 1976.

Mason, Kathy. *Natural Museums: United States National Parks, 1872–1916*. East Lansing: Michigan State Press, 2004.

Maswoud, S. Javed. "Kakadu and the Politics of World Heritage Listing." *Australian Journal of International Affairs* 54:2 (2000), 357–370.

Maoz, D., and Bekerman, Z. "Searching for Jewish Answers in Indian Resorts: The Postmodern Traveler." *Annals of Tourism Research* 37:2 (2010), 423–439.

Minca, Claudo, and Tim Oakes (eds.). *Travels in Paradox: Remapping Tourism*. Lanham, MD: Rowman & Littlefield, 2006.

Musitelli, Jean. "2002 World Heritage, Between Universalism and Globalization." *International Journal of Cultural Property* 11:2 (2002), 323–336.

Naquin, Susan, and Yu Chun-Fang (eds.). "Introduction." In *Pilgrims and Sacred Sites in China* (pp. 1–38). Berkeley: University of California Press, 1992.

Nash, Roderick. *Wilderness and the American Mind*. New London: Yale University Press, 1967.

Naughton, Barry. "Danwei: The Economic Foundations of a Unique Institution." In Lu Xiaobo and Elizabeth Perry (eds.), *Danwei: The Changing Chinese Workplace in Historical and Comparative Perspective* (pp. 169–194). Armonk, NY: M.E. Sharpe 1997.

Nicholson, Marjorie. *Mountain Gloom and Mountain Glory: The Development of the Aesthetics of the Infinite*. New York: W.W. Norton & Company, 1959.

Nolan, Mary Lee, and Sidney Nolan. "Religious Sites as Tourism Attractions in Europe." *Annals of Tourism Research* 19:1 (1992), 68–78.

Norton, Bryan. "Environmental Ethics and Weak Anthropocentrism." In Andrew Light and Holmes Rolston (eds.), *Environmental Ethics: An Anthology* (pp. 163–174). Oxford, England: Blackwell Publishers, 2003.

Notar. Beth. *Displacing Desire: Travel and Popular Culture in China*. Honolulu: University of Hawaii Press, 2006.

Nuryanti, Wiendu. "Heritage and Postmodern Tourism." *Annals of Tourism Research* 23:2 (1996), 249–260.

Nyíri, Pal. *Scenic Spots: Chinese Tourism, the State, and Cultural Authenticity*. Seattle: University of Washington, 2006a.

——— "The Yellow Man's Burden: Chinese Migrants on a Civilizing Mission." *The Asian Journal* 56 (July 2006b), 83–106.

——— "Between Encouragement and Control: Tourism, Modernity and Discipline in China." In Tim Winter, Peggy Teo, and T. C. Chang (eds.), *Asia on Tour: Exploring the Rise of Asian Tourism* (pp. 153–169). London: Routledge, 2009.

Oakes, Timothy. "Ethnic Tourism in Rural Guizhou: Sense of Place and the Commerce of Authenticity." In Michel Picard and Robert Wood (eds.), *Tourism, Ethnicity, and the State in Asian and Pacific Societies* (pp. 35–70). Honolulu: University of Hawai'i Press, 1997.

———*Tourism and Modernity in China*. New York: Routledge, 1998.

Oakes, Tim, and Donald Sutton (eds.). *Faiths on Display: Religion, Tourism, and the Chinese State*. Lanham, MD: Rowman & Littlefield, 2010.

Olson, Daniel. "Management Issues for Religious Heritage Attractions." In Dallen J. Timothy and Daniel Olson (eds.), *Tourism, Religion and Spiritual Journeys* (pp. 104–118). New York: Routledge Press, 2006.

Patin, Valery. "Will Market Forces Rule?" In Sagarika Dutt (ed.), *UNESCO and a Just World Order* (pp. 138–140). New York: NOVA Science Publishing, 2002.

Reader, Ian, and Walter, Thomas (eds.). *Pilgrimage in Popular Culture*. New York: MacMillan Press, 1993.

Roberts, Dexter. "China's Spiritual Awakening." *Business Week*, January 10, 2008. Accessed January 16, 2012: http://www.businessweek.com/magazine/content/08_03/b4067050290718.htm

Rogaski, Ruth. *Hygienic Modernity: Meanings of Health and Disease in Treaty Port China*. Berkeley: University of California Press, 2004.

Rolston, Holmes. "Value in Nature and the Nature of Value." In Andrew Light and Holmes Rolston (eds.), *Environmental Ethics: An Anthology* (pp. 143–153). Oxford, England: Blackwell Publishers, 2003.

Rioux, Yu Luo. "Pilgrim or Tourist? The Transformation of China's Revolutionary Holy Land." In Tim Oake and Donald Sutton (eds.), *Faiths on Display: Religion, Tourism, and the Chinese State* (pp. 79–102). Lanham, MD: Rowman & Littlefield, 2010.

Ryan, Chris, and Gu Huimin. "Constructionism and Culture in Research: Understandings of the Fourth Buddhist Festival, Wutaishan, China." *Tourism Management* 31:2 (2009), 167–178.

Sagoff, Mark. "Can Environmentalists be Liberals?" In Robert Elliot (ed.), *Environmental Ethics* (pp. 165–187). Oxford and New York: Oxford University Press, 1995.

Santos, Xose. "Pilgrimage and Tourism at Santiago de Compostela." *Tourism Recreation Research* 27:2 (2002), 41–50.

Scott, James C. *Seeing Like a State: How Certain Schemes to Improve the Human Condition Have Failed.* New Haven, CT: Yale University Press, 1998.

Sewell, James. *UNESCO and World Politics.* Princeton, NJ: Princeton University Press, 1975.

Shackley, Myra. "Managing the Cultural Impacts of religious Tourism in the Himalayas, Tibet and Nepal." In Michael Robinson and Priscilla Boniface (eds.), *Tourism and Cultural Conflicts* (pp. 95–112). Wallingford, UK: University of Northumbria Press, 1999.

——— "Space, Sanctity and Service: The English Cathedral as *Heterotopia.*" *International Journal of Tourism Research* 4:5 (2002), 345–352.

Shapiro, Judith. *Mao's War against Nature: Politics and the Environment in Revolutionary China.* Cambridge, England: Cambridge University Press, 2001.

Shepherd, Robert. "Commodification, Culture and Tourism." *Tourist Studies* 2:2 (2002), 183–201.

———*When Culture goes to Market: Space, Place, and Identity in an Urban Marketplace.* New York: Peter Lang, 2008.

Silverman, Helaine, and D. Fairchild Ruggles (eds.). *Cultural Heritage and Human Rights.* New York: Springer Press, 2007a.

———"Cultural Heritage and Human Rights." In *Cultural Heritage and Human Rights.* New York: Springer Press, 2007b, 3–22.

66,000 shimin yonghegong jinxiang xinfu ("66,000 People Line up at Yonghegong to Burn Incense for Good Fortune"), *Beijing News*, February, 4, 2011. Accessed August 15, 2011: http://news.bjnews.com.cn/2011/0204/107514.shtml

Slayter, Ralph. *World Heritage.* Stockholm: Swedish Academy of Sciences, 1983.

Smith, Laurajane. "Empty gestures? Heritage and the Politics of Recognition." In Helaine Silverman and D. Fairchild Ruggles (eds.), *Cultural Heritage and Human Rights* (pp. 159–171). New York: Springer Press, 2007.

Sober, Elliot. "Philosophical Problems for Environmentalism." In Robert Elliot (ed.), *Environmental Ethics* (pp. 226–247.). Oxford and New York: Oxford University Press, 1995.

Sofield, Trevor, and Fung Mei Li. "Tourism Development and Cultural Policies in China." *Annals of Tourism Research* 25:2 (1998), 362–392.

Su Hong. *Wu Ye Miao: Lifo, Qiyi, Yi Ben Biao* [Wuye Temple: A Guide to Buddhist Prayer and Temple Manners]. Hohot: Inner Mongolia Peoples Publishing House, 2006.

Su Xiaobo, and Peggy Teo. *The Politics of Heritage Tourism in China: A View from Lijiang.* London: Routledge, 2009.

Šulc, Branka. "The Protection of Croatia's Cultural Heritage during War 1991–1995." In Robert Layton, Julian Thomas, and Peter Stone (eds.), *Destruction and Conservation of Cultural Property* (pp. 157–167). London: Routledge, 2001.

Timothy, D. J., and D. H. Olsen. (2006). "Tourism and Religious Journeys." In D. J. Timothy and D. H. Olsen (eds.), *Tourism, Religion and Spiritual Journeys* (pp. 1–21). London: Routledge, 2006.

Timothy, D. J., and Gyan Nyaupane (eds.). *Cultural Heritage and Tourism in the Developing World: A Regional Perspective.* London: Routledge Press, 2009.

Tomba, Luigi. "Of Quality, Harmony, and Community: Civilization and the Middle Class in Urban China." *Positions* 17:3 (2009), 591–616.

Tuohy, Sue. "Cultural Metaphors and Reasoning." *Asian Folklore Studies* 50 (1991), 189–220.

Turner, Victor, and Edith Turner. *Image and Pilgrimage in Christian Culture*. New York: Columbia University Press, 1978.

Tuttle, Gray. *Tibetan Buddhists in the Making of Modern China*. New York: Columbia University Press, 2005.

UNESCO. "Convention Concerning the Protection of the World Cultural and Natural Heritage" (1972): http://www.Unesco.org

UNESCO. "Evaluation Report: Mount Wutai (China), No. 1279." Paris: ICOMOS, March 10, 2009.

UNESCO. Intergovernmental Committee for the Protection of the World Cultural and Natural Heritage. *Operational Guidelines for the Implementation of the World Heritage Convention*. Paris: UNESCO World Heritage Centre, January 2008a.

UNESCO. *Our Creative Diversity: Report of the World Commission on Culture and Development*. Paris: Unesco Publishing House, 1995.

UNESCO. "Tentative World Heritage List: Mount Wutai Administrative Bureau," 2008b Accessed January 7, 2012: http://www.whc.unesco.org/en/tentativelists/1621/

UNESCO. World Heritage Committee, 26th Session, Budapest, Hungary, June 24–29, 2002. Accessed January 7, 2012: http://whc.unesco.org/en/sessions/26COM

UNESCO. World Heritage Committee, 29th Session, Durban, South Africa, July 10–17, 2005.

UNESCO. World Heritage List: Lhasa, Case NO 707: Advisory Body Evaluation, 26 October, 1993. Accessed January 10, 2012: http://whc.unesco.org/archive/advisory_body_evaluation/707ter.pdf

UNESCO. *World Heritage Sites: A Complete Guide to 890 UNESCO World Heritage Sites*. Paris: UNESCO Publishing House, 2010.

Uvin, Peter. *Aiding Violence: The Development Enterprise in Rwanda*. New York: Kumarian Press, 1998.

Vukonic, Boris. *Tourism and Religion*. New York: Pergamon Press, 1992.

Wang Yaping, Wang Yunlin, and Glen Bramler. "Chinese Housing Reform in State-owned Enterprises and Its Impact on Different Social Groups." *Urban Studies* 42:10 (2005), 1859–1878.

Wei, Julia Lee, Ramon Myers, and Donald Gillin (eds.). *Prescriptions for Saving China: Selected Writings of Sun Yatsen*. Stanford, CA: Hoover Institution Press, 1994.

Weller, Robert. *Discovering Nature: Globalization and Environmental Culture in China and Taiwan*. Cambridge, England: Cambridge University Press, 2006.

Wilkins, Thurman. *John Muir: Apostle of Nature*. Norman: University of Oklahoma Press, 1995.

Winter, Tim. "Rethinking Tourism in Asia." *Annals of Tourism Research* 34:1 (2007), 27–44.

Winter, Michael, and Ruth Gasson. "Pilgrimage and Tourism: Cathedral Visiting in Contemporary England." *International Journal of Heritage Studies* 2:3 (1996), 172–182.

Womack, Brantly. "Transfigured Community: Neo-Traditionalism and Work-Unit Socialism in China." *China Quarterly* 126 (June 1991), 313–332.

Xie, Philip Feifan. *Authenticating Ethnic Tourism*. Buffalo, NY: Channel View Publications, 2010.

Xinhua. "China Issues New Regulations on House Expropriation." January 22, 2011. Accessed July 20, 2011: http://www.chinadaily.com.cn/china/2011-01/22/content_11900647.htm

Xu, Jian. "Body, Discourse and the Cultural Politics of Contemporary Chinese Qigong." *Journal of Asian Studies* 58:4 (1999), 961–991.

Yan Hairong. "Neoliberal Governmentality *and* Neohumanism: Organizing Suzhi/Value Flow through Labor Recruitment Networks." *Cultural Anthropology* 18:4 (2003), 493–523.

Yang, Mayfair. "Tradition, Traveling Anthropology and the Discourse of Modernity in China." In Henrietta Moore (ed.), *The Future of Anthropology* (pp. 93–114). New York: Routledge, 1996.

Yao Xinyong. "Religious Belief and Practice in Urban China 1995–2005." *Journal of Contemporary Religion* 22:2 (2007), 169–185.

Yip Ka-Che. "Health and Nationalist Reconstruction: Health in Nationalist China, 1928–1937." *Modern Asian Studies* 26:2 (1992), 395–415.

Zhang Haiyang. "Wrestling with the Connotations of Chinese 'Minzu.'" *Economic and Political Weekly*, July 26, 1997, 74–84.

Zhang Li. *Strangers in the City: Reconfigurations of Space, Power, and Social Networks within China's Floating Population*. Palo Alto, CA: Stanford University Press, 2004.

Zhang Mu, Huang Li, Wang Jianhong, Liu Ji, Jie Yangeng, and Lai Xiting, "Religious Tourism and Cultural Pilgrimage: A Chinese Perspective." In R. Raj and N. D. Morpeth (eds.), *Religious Tourism and Pilgrimage Management: An Alternative Perspective* (pp. 98–112.). Cambridge, MA: CABI Publishing, 2007.

Zhang Qian. *China's Ethnic Groups and Religion*. Beijing: China International Press, 2010.

Zhang Xing Quan. *Privatization: A Study of Housing Policy in Urban China*. New York: Nova Science Publications, 1998.

Zhuang Min. "The Administration of China's Archeological Heritage." In Henry Cleere (ed.), *Archeological Heritage Management in the Modern World* (pp. 102–109). Oxford, England: Uwin Hyman, 1989.

Zhuangzi (trans. Wang Rongpei). Changsha: Hunan People's Publishing House, 1999.

INDEX

Page numbers appearing in italics refer to photographs and tables are noted with an italicized *t* following the page number.

About the Author

Robert Shepherd is Assistant Professor of Anthropology and International Affairs at the George Washington University in Washington, DC, where he teaches courses on contemporary Chinese culture and society, the anthropology of development, and human rights. His research interests include tourism practices, moral frameworks of marketplace behavior, and the construction of cultural heritage in postcolonial societies. Originally from Buffalo, New York, he has served in the United States Peace Corps in rural Nepal, worked on United Nations Development Program projects in China and Indonesia, and taught in Taiwan. He is the author of *When Culture Goes to Market: Space, Place and Identity in an Urban Marketplace* (2008) and *Partners in Paradise: Tourism Practices, Heritage Policies, and Anthropological Sites* (2011).

About the Author